Farmers

From Food Producers
to
Park-Keepers

Arthur Staniforth

Note for Librarians: A cataloguing record for this book is available from Library and Archives Canada at www.collectionscanada.ca/amicus/index-e.html
ISBN 1-4120-5534-2

Printed in Victoria, BC, Canada. Printed on paper with minimum 30% recycled fibre. Trafford's print shop runs on "green energy" from solar, wind and other environmentally-friendly power sources.

PUBLISHING™
Offices in Canada, USA, Ireland and UK
This book was published on-demand in cooperation with Trafford Publishing. On-demand publishing is a unique process and service of making a book available for retail sale to the public taking advantage of on-demand manufacturing and Internet marketing. On-demand publishing includes promotions, retail sales, manufacturing, order fulfilment, accounting and collecting royalties on behalf of the author.

Book sales for North America and international:
Trafford Publishing, 6E–2333 Government St.,
Victoria, BC v8t 4p4 CANADA
phone 250 383 6864 (toll-free 1 888 232 4444)
fax 250 383 6804; email to orders@trafford.com
Book sales in Europe:
Trafford Publishing (UK) Limited, 9 Park End Street, 2nd Floor
Oxford, UK oxi ihh UNITED KINGDOM
phone 44 (0)1865 722 113 (local rate 0845 230 9601)
facsimile 44 (0)1865 722 868; info.uk@trafford.com
Order online at:
trafford.com/05-0432

10 9 8 7 6 5 4 3 2

Acknowledgements

My first words must go to my parents who managed to continue farming the D'Urbans Farm through the years of deep agricultural depression and to provide their four children with a wonderful upbringing and to see them through their school education.

With the manuscript of this book, I have had much help from my wife, Mary, and from my sister Patricia and daughter-in-law Lindsay and from Tom Worthington of Reading Agricultural Consultants: they have been through the typescript and have made many useful suggestions. My son, Robin, has given invaluable assistance in working my personal computer.

My thanks are due also to Edmund Brown for up-to-date information about farming in Framlingham parish. I have also had support from Muriel Kilvert whose book, A History of Framlingham, has provided much background information. Bob Roberts, editor of FRAM, the Journal of the Framlingham & District Local History & Preservation Society, has given my book most useful backing. Cedric Pulford, of the Ituri Press, has been very helpful in preparation for publication.

The author also thanks the Lincolnshire Echo, the Farmers Weekly, DEFRA [MAFF as was], the Oxfordshire Times, the British Library and Reading University Museum of Rural Life for the use of illustrations, as attributed.

Foreword

Long shelves of books tell us about the changes that have come upon farming in the 20th century, but there will never be another one quite like this, for the author has to have reached a certain age to be able to speak with first hand experience of the first part of the century- a crucial time to compare with today. So this book is very important as a record of events in the English countryside It is also very readable, for the story is plainly told, and the best stories need no literary embellishments.

In the 1920s the farmer was a food producer, today he has become a supplier of raw materials to the food manufacturing industry which depends upon four or five supermarket companies. But the farmer is not even at the beginning of the food chain as he used to be, subject to the help of his blacksmith and wheelwright, because now he cannot start a day's work without being supplied or serviced by many others who may live thousands of miles away, extracting his phosphate in Senegal or rubber in Malaysia. Once parochial, the food business has become globalised, putting the farmer somewhere in the middle of the food chain. It has made him very vulnerable.

Our author's boyhood was spent in East Anglia, so he saw the depression from the perspective of the arable sector. My memories of the 1930s is of livestock and life was kinder. It bore out the old saying, "Down corn, up horn" and vice versa. Poorer soil and more rain in the western half of our country made it sensible to put the fields down to grass and embark on dairying to supply the towns with their daily pints. Internal combustion in the form of the milk lorry made it possible for milk from the cow in Devonshire to reach even London, via the new milk trains travelling through the night, to be delivered the following morning on any doorstep in the metropolis. Yet only a few years previously, in the 1920s, you could still see a cow in the West End milked beside the pavement. Throughout the inter-war years, the farm gate price of milk averaged 1s 0d a gallon, and a manual showed that one could earn £1,000 a year with only 30 cows on 80 acres, and I went off to be a pupil on such a farm, valued at £25 an acre.

Arthur Staniforth tells us of the repeal of the Corn Production Act in 1921. We should never forget what happened then. Between 1922 and 1936 when the Wheat Act was passed, the average farm gate price of wheat was 10s 2d a hundredweight. In today's money and metric language, that is well over £300 a tonne, a several times better price than today; and on the face of it, the Staniforth family should have been very rich and David, the horseman, on a good wage. The comparison, though, must be qualified. The yield on D'Urbans land would have been about 20 cwt per acre at best, and it is now three or four times as much.

So there is a very important lesson to be drawn from this book. Government intervention introduced price support systems; these were a signal for research into ways to increase output by raising productivity per animal and per acre, but as this productivity rose, so farm gate prices fell. The input/output ratio went up and to pay for all the extra inputs needed, the farmer began to borrow even more money from the banks.

In the 1920s and 1930s and even until the 1960s it was usual for a son to follow the father into farming. Throughout those years and even back to Napoleonic times there had been approximately the same number of farmers - 500,000, give or take a few thousands. Now it is a fraction of that number. What a tragedy! Support prices have not supported farmers. But has the the total number of people in the chain of food production changed? We know from the census figures it was 2,000,000 when the chain was extremely short in Arthur Staniforth's boyhood; now that it is extremely long the number is probably much the same, except that many are unaware that they are an indispensable part of modern farming.

Let's be optimistic. Electronic gadgetry is going to enable another 10 million people now with jobs in our cities and conurbation's to do the same work far away in the countryside. Having made their escape I suspect a large number will join the many who already break off from their computers and go out to a few acres with their goats or pigs or poultry or even a modest arable crop. Surpluses from them already are going to farmers' markets for direct sale to the consumer. Here is a parallel food chain, and as short as it was in the 1920s. There is a difference; this yeomanry of the 21st century will control their market for their income will not depend upon it.

Arthur Staniforth, however, did not follow on the farm. No doubt he is glad that he didn't, and his readers will be glad too. No one else could have had quite the same mix of experiences as he has had. They have enabled him to give us a book that should take its place on the shelf of every farmer and of those of the few remaining colleges where agriculture is taught.

Sir Richard Body

Introduction

There are two main sections to this book. The first covers the author's youth in the inter-war years on his father's farm, the D'Urbans, Framlingham, Suffolk. This takes us from the expansive era of the first world war, through the years of depression and neglect until the late 1930's when a further war loomed and it could be seen that home food production might again become important.

The second part of the book deals with farming during and after the second world war when the author worked for the Ministry of Agriculture, Fisheries and Food [MAFF]. This period saw an extraordinary reversal in public attitude to farming and the industry was showered with a plethora of production grants and subsidies.

British farming became highly efficient. Production soared while prices were kept under control. The book ends at a time when obesity is a greater national problem than food shortage and agricultural production is far less important than protection of the environment for birds and wild plants.

Ever since society became divided between food producers and the rest, there has been an uneasy relationship between the two sides. Shakespeare wrote his snide comment on the farmer who hanged himself in the expectation of plenty - but he did not say whether this was because the unfortunate cultivator feared low prices or the pitiful esteem in which he would shortly be held.

1

A Start in Farming

My father farmed, before and during the first world war, a small farm of about 100 acres, the Oaks Farm, in the parish of Framlingham, Suffolk - so named because there were around the yard a cluster of ancient surivals of the medieval oak forests. There seem to be few remaining records of my parents' life and work at the Oaks during the first world war. I was not on the scene at that time but my father told of an episode that occurred during the period of obsessional spy mania that gripped the population in eastern England. Night watchers on the tower of St. Michael's church detected a light flashing at intervals in the distance, and they trained a telescope on the offending spot. It turned out to be the Oaks Farm and my parents had to explain that it was the opening and shutting of the back door that had caused the signal to the enemy.

One other reminder of those times which came to light in an old bureau drawer is the partly used ration book pictured below.

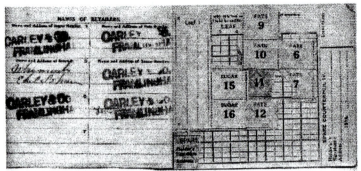

RATION BOOK FROM THE FIRST WORLD WAR,
WITH SOME SUGAR AND FATS STILL TO CLAIM

The years between 1910 and 1920 were a time of recovery for farming after the depression of the late Victorian and Edwardian era. Shipping losses in the first world war reduced the nation's bread and food reserves to about six weeks supply and, in order to encourage home agriculture, the government, in 1917, passed the Corn Production Act which guaranteed cereal prices as well as supporting farm wages

On the strength of this, my father bought the neighboring 186-acre D'Urbans farm at the prevailing high price in 1920. He was to pay for this, in high mortgage costs throughout the depression years.

I was born there in the sunny summer of 1921 but this auspicious event coincided with the repeal of the Corn Production Act and the beginning of a period of steep decline in farming. The Journal of the Ministry of Agriculture {October, 1922} reported the minister, Sir Arthur Boscawen, as saying that 'All industries are depressed today, but agriculture is probably the most depressed of all.' Mike Soper, in his book, 'Years of Change', [Farming Press, 1995] says, in reference to the repeal of the Corn Production Act, *The result was catastrophic. Within two years the price of wheat was halved and many bankruptcies followed, not least among the many ex-servicemen who had invested their gratuities in small farms. To farmers with long memories, the repeal of the Corn Production Act still stands as an extreme example of government perfidy.*

Another quote, from John Cherrington's autobiography, 'On the Smell of an Oily Rag', [Farming Press, 1979], points up the situation in which my father found himself. *Of course, I have been very lucky. ..... I have not known anything of a permanent downturn, unlike those unfortunates who came in, say, in 1919 or 1920.*

There was also the matter of tithe. To this day I do not know how my father dealt with the tithe charge on the farm. Tithe on land has a very long and convoluted history. A much simplified description of the charge would be that it required landowners to pay one tenth of their harvest to the established church for the maintenance of churches and the payment of stipends. The few remaining tithe barns that dot the countryside are surviving evidence of the old system. By the time we farmed at the D'Urbans, tithe had become a straight financial charge on farm land, often calculated in abstruse ways. There was countrywide resistance to paying an anachronistic tax. Many in the church sympathised. A bishop is quoted in Carol Twinch's book, 'Tithe War', [Old Pond], 2001, as saying in a sermon at Cuddesdon College, in 1935, 'Can you wonder that farmers who bought their land on a mortgage, at a time of inflated prices, should, in a period of depression, feel bitter about paying the tithe that was stabilised during the time of those inflated prices?' Farmers who could not, or would not, pay the charge had their farms invaded by bailiffs who seized livestock or other moveable assets to be sold on the spot in distraint sales. The tithe war against the establishment was extraordinarily long drawn out, and all forms of this tax have only recently been extinguished.

2

The D'Urbans Farm

THE D'URBANS FARM

We often wondered how the D'Urbans Farm acquired its romantic name and it was only recently that the explanation came to light in a June 1995 number of the East Anglian Daily Times. It got the name early in the nineteenth century when the farm was part of an estate owned by Dr John D'Urban of Halesworth in the county of Suffolk - whose son, Sir Benjamin D'Urban, became Governor of the Cape of Good Hope from

1834 to 1837 and after whom the Natal port of Durban was named The family subsequently dropped the apostrophe from their name which now survives only at the farm.

The cream-washed, pargeted farmhouse was situated on a hill, or what passed for a hill in that gently undulating landscape. The pargeting, or decorated plaster work, gave an indication of the age of the house, the walls of which were constructed of a timber framework infilled with clay lump. These walls had been covered with lime plaster strengthened with hair and craftsmen had worked the decorations into the plaster. - but this pargeting exists no longer since the whole front of the house has recently been replastered. There are surviving examples in Suffolk of the technique which was widely practised in the 16th and 17th centuries.

The oak timbers would have been cut at a time when the area was noted for its fine oak woods. John Evelyn, in his 'Discourse on Forest Trees' [1664], quoted by Muriel Kilvert,* praised Framlingham, for 'its magnificent oaks, the finest in the world'. The seventeenth century warship, Royal Sovereign, the flagship of King Charles II's navy, was built of Framlingham oak.

From the upstairs windows we looked east, in company with the house-martins that returned every year to nest under the eaves, to the little town of Framlingham with the flint stone tower of St Michael's church, about a mile away. As well as the church service peals and the mournful tolling for funerals, there was the occasional great clanging to call the firemen to their station. Every four hours in the nineteen twenties and thirties, the church bells played Home Sweet Home and, when the easterly breeeze was blowing, there would drift across the sound of bells from the village church at Dennington, surely the sweetest peal in England. A sound that would come in through my bedroom window on a summer's morning was the splashing of the horses as they came down for their early morning drink at the horse pond. There was a shallow, gravel bottomed entrance at one end of the pond and they loved to splash themselves with their forefeet when the weather was warm.

One other sound that comes to mind when thinking of those days was the cheerful jangling of the Cambridge roll - or rib-roll as it was called

* Muriel Kilvert. History of Framlingham, Bolton & Price, 1995

in Suffolk. The Cambridge roll [named after the man who invented it] consists of a series of heavy iron rings threaded on a spindle with enough play between them to allow them to jostle each other so that they jangle pleasantly as the roll is pulled over the land.

It was my good fortune to be born and brought up at the D'Urbans Farm. There were many other farms of moderate size in East Suffolk but the D'Urbans was one of the most attractive. Although it was at a time of deep agricultural depression in arable farming, to me it was a wonderful place in which to grow up.

A small stream, the beginning of the river Ore, ran down the northern side, bordered by a thin, straggly wood. This was called the Gull and it provided a fine home for wild life - or 'habitat' as the environmentalists would now call it. Rabbits in particular loved the pockets of glacial sand and gravel which were interspersed in the boulder clay, and many sorts of birds nested in the trees and bushes. Dairmaid O'Muirithe, writing in The Oldie, October 1999, says, 'gill, from old Norse gil, a steep glen with a stream at the bottom' - this may explain the name 'Gull'.

The layout of the fields in the twenties and thirties was the same as that shown on the 1906 Ordnance Survey map and can have changed little since Victorian times. The 23 fields, all within a ring fence, gave a total acreage of 186. The biggest was the 14-acre and the average size was just over 8 acres. Every field had a name; Pond field was so named because it had the pond at its corner which supplied water for four cottages, all of it drawn in buckets. Gravel Pits had the pit at its eastern end which provided sand when we needed it and a nesting place for the sand martins that returned every year. Stonelands was at the other end of the farm where there must have been a terminal moraine at the end of the ice age.

The origin of the name of the farm has been established. But who was Will who gave his name to Will's Hill? And why was Nettus Arms so called? We had a Neathouse [pronounced Nettus] to house 'neat' stock, or young stock, on the farm alongside the horse stable, but could there have been a public house at the corner of the farm, at its west end, to serve a cluster of houses between Framlingham and Earl Soham? These are idle speculations because the names have now gone for ever in amalgamations, a loss that must have been repeated all over the country, particularly in the arable east where mechanisation rules.

The small fields were well adapted to cultivation by horses - of which we originally had eight. But they were all separated by hedges and ditches extending to a total length of two or three miles. In our first years at the farm, with four full-time men, it was possible to keep the hedges tidy and the arable field borders mowed by scythe every year. But, as the price of wheat tumbled in the twenties and thirties my father had to reduce the regular labour force to two and the finer points of farming went by the board. To quote the chairman of the Wheat Commission, Earl Peel, ' .... *everyone knows that .... the world price of wheat is so low that it is hardly possible anywhere in the country to cultivate it at a profit'*.

This may be a good point at which to say something about scythes. As with the flail for threshing, we were among the last to use the scythe for cutting corn at harvest. We had to do this when our binder was drawn by horses which would have badly trampled the standing crop when making the first cut round the field headland. The first cut, 'opening up' as it was called, was done with the scythe and the cut corn was bound into sheaves with long corn stalks and moved to the headland out of the path of the horses. We must have cut a few acres in this way in the course of a harvest season, and it was very hard work.

Some have waxed lyrical about scything and it can indeed give satisfaction to swing a well-set, well-sharpened scythe over a small area. William Deedes, at age 90, writing in the Daily Telegraph of 7.7.03, laments the passing of the 'cigar' shaped carborundum rub for sharpening scythes, '.... *bad news for those of us who like scything -*

CUTTING WITH THE SCYTHE AND BINDING BY HAND. MERL.

I use the lighter turk version these days. Scything works wonders for the waistline. Denied the stones to sharpen scythes, we are doomed to become even more obese.'

Prime Minister Stanley Baldwin in a

speech in 1924 extolled the sights and sounds of England '..... *the sound of the scythe against the whetstone, and the sight of a plough team coming over the brow of a hill ....*'

But to harvest thousands of acres in this way, as was done before the arrival of the binder, must have been an enormous labour.

Matthew Arnold describes, with sibilant alliteration, a gang of mowers, seen by students rowing on the Thames, as they '*stood with suspended scythes to see us pass*'. One can be sure that the mowers were glad to have the excuse to straighten their backs for a few minutes to watch the young gentlemen row by.

There were nominally five cottages on the farm of which two, semi-detached and of poor lath-and-plaster construction, were unoccupied for most of our time. Frank, the foreman, and Sam Banthorpe, his brother, occupied a pair of small, brick-built single storied cottages with their old father and mother; while David Smith, the horseman and his wife and two sons lived in another small, brick-built cottage. I only saw the inside of these cottages once or twice; they were primitively equipped. You went upstairs in David's cottage by way of a ladder with a rail. It hardly needs saying that none had a bathroom or bath. However, all had large, productive vegetable gardens, manured from time to time with muck from the farm, and space to store the farm-cut firewood which was their main fuel supply. The cottages were rent free and they have long since disappeared.

There were no other young children on our neighbours' farms. Major and Mrs Rolfe had two grown-up sons. Mr Brown, a retired clothier and a 'gentleman farmer' lived with his sister at Red House Farm , Kettleborough; and Jack Priest now farmed the neighbouring Oaks Farm. He was a rough type with no known antecedents and no apparent relations or friends - a true recluse. The other adjoining farm was occupied by John Larter who had no children. Even in those days this farm was too small to provide a living and Mr Larter had a second business - it would now be called 'diversification' - in organising the procurement of pigs for the bacon factory, and he is listed as 'livestock agent' as well as 'farmer' in Kelly's directory, 1937.

There were numerous public houses in Framlingham and a variety of places of worship, including St Michael's Church and the Methodist, Congregational and Unitarian chapels, Canon Lanchester, a benevolent, white-haired figure - was vicar of the parish church and he would cycle out to the farm on occasion and take tea with my mother. There was no telephone so she could not have known when he would push his bicycle up the driveway, but she seemed always to have some scones or Suffolk rusks and of course some home-made jam to put on the table. We seldom went the mile or so to church, but when we did, it was more likely to be to the Methodist church which was considerably nearer to the farm than St Michael's.

Making some sort of a living by keeping a few livestock was commoner in those days. We would often see half-a-dozen dairy cows, tended by a girl from a smallholding on the other side of Rolfe's farm, on the wide verges of nearby roads and lanes. It was free grazing and there was little traffic to disturb the peaceful scene.

3

Life on the Farm

Four ponds had been dug into the boulder clay around the farmhouse. One provided the domestic water supply, via a pipe to the big hand pump that stood beside the stone scullery sink. We used to fill the wood-fired copper by hand on wash days. Another pipe led from the copper to the bathroom above where a small rotary hand-pump was used to fill the enamelled bath.

During one or two very dry summers the water in the partly dried up domestic water pond would turn a pinkish colour, with algal growth. Often it happened that, when we had visitors or guests who considered such matters to be important, we had to cycle down to the town, where there was a reliable well with a big hand pump from which we could fill our cans with drinking water. We had no car in those days and my mother's bicycle, with solid rubber tyres, acetylene lamp and back-pedal brake, was our best wheeled mode of transport.

THE SPRING PUMP - NOTE THE TWO SPOUTS.

The Spring Pump, as it was called, was the only reliable source of potable water for many households in the parish until after World War II. The pump had an upper handle and spout which were used to fill containers carried on carts.

There was a big rainwater tank at the back of the D'Urbans farm house which supplied soft water for clothes washing. We were careful to turn the tap off tightly so that the rain water did not run to waste, but this supply dried up in a long rainless spell.

For milk, we had Daisy, the Jersey cow, and as a small boy I would bring her in, in the morning, from the orchard to the cow-house where my father milked her. When Daisy was no more, we got our milk from the Rolfes' farm or from the Browns' Hill Farm, next door, in cans, again by bicycle. In the town, milk was still being delivered in churns carried on a yoke and dispensed to customers by pint measures. Hygiene? There was no compulsory tuberculin testing in those days and tuberculosis, or 'consumption' as it was called, was much commoner than today.

There was, however, one aspect of housekeeping on the farm seventy years ago that compares favourably with modern practice. Every Friday Mr Gray from Carley's grocery would ring the front door bell and he and my mother would sit down at the mahogany dining table and make out the week's list of groceries that

THE AUTHOR BRINGING DAISY IN FOR MILKING. FAMILY PHOTOGRAPH.

would be delivered without fail on the following Tuesday. Supermarkets and the internet have brought no great improvement, unless it is in the plethora of choice which they offer. We would also buy a few items from time to time, in Carley's shop itself and the girl at the check-out, as we would now call it, would put our bill, with prices marked and the money to pay, in a small container which she whizzed on a taut wire to the cashier in his office, across the shop, whence it would be whizzed back with receipt and change.

There was a yard at the back of the farmhouse where firewood was stored. There would be twenty or thirty faggots for kindling and a good pile of long timber to be cut up for the log fires that kept us warm in the cold East Anglian winters.

We had, of course, no electricity or gas on the farm. There was a cast iron, wood-fired bread oven in the kitchen but it was hardly ever used. Two other pieces of Victorian equipment were the wringer and mangle which were regularly used. The washing, after it had been put through the wringer, was carried a hundred yards to the clothes line at the end of the garden. It was a long line and needed a basket full of pegs. These pegs were of split willow, held together with thin bands of tin round their tops; they were made by gypsies who sold them at the door. It all seems unbelievably laborious in this era of automatic washing machines and tumble-driers. However, we did have paraffin in those days and my mother did most of the cooking in a paraffin-fuelled Florence stove with oven.

Another relic of the Victorian way of life was the small, detached stone hut at the north end of the farmhouse. This was the privy . Until I was about ten years old this operated as a simple cess pit but my father decided that it needed modernisation. He concreted over the floor and installed a lavatory bucket beneath the seat. The contents had, of course, to be emptied and dug into the vegetable garden from time to time - an unpopular task. Having no running water in the house meant that we could not move the further step and put in a W C with a septic tank. The town of Framlingham was no more advanced than we were in this matter and had no modern sewage system until after the second world war - see Muriel Kilvert.

How did we exist in the hot summer months without a refrigerator? All we had in the kitchen was a larder with perforated zinc sides. Milk soon went off; my mother made scones with sour milk and, when the scones were likely to go stale, they were split and baked again to make Suffolk rusks which would keep for some time in a tin. I think we had more soup in those days, too, because chicken carcases or other meat could not be kept for long.

The mincing machine was regularly used and the jars of potted meat, topped with clarified butter, were one of our delicacies. better than any of the array of savoury spreads now offered by the supermarkets. The refrigerator can be blamed for the virtual disappearance of potted meat.

THE INGLENOOK FIREPLACE: NOTE THE WARMING PAN AND QUOITS BOARD.

In cold weather we would sit round our ingle-nooked open fire in the living room. The old house was extraordinarily draughty and when the wind blew. the heavy curtain strung between the living room and the scullery door would shiver and shake as if at sea. The timber frame of the house would creak in a really strong easterly gale, but a plantation of big chestnut trees gave us shelter on our western side. My sister and I would sit on the inglenook seats, sometimes watching and turning the big yellow bowl of dough as it rose in the hearth before the fire.

We had an Aladdin paraffin lamp for reading downstairs at night and it gave a good light provided the wick was regularly trimmed so that no soot collected on the mantle. Candles were the order of the day when we went upstairs or to other rooms in the dark, and you had to shield the flame with your hand in the draughty stairways and corridors. The fireplaces in the bedrooms were used very occasionally if we were ill in cold weather; and hot water bottles or sometimes the warming pan were used to warm the beds. Rubber hot water bottles came in in the thirties but it has taken many more years for the ultimate bed warmer for the effete - the electric blanket - to come to our aid.

As we sat round the fire at night, my father would read the Daily News {later the News Chronicle} or travel books and sometimes when I was small, stories from old volumes of the Boys Own Paper - stories such as 'How we beat the Druses', or 'The Cock House at Felsgarth'. I soon began to read R M Ballantyne books like 'The Young Fur Traders' or 'The Gorilla Hunters', or seafaring stories such as 'Two Years Before the Mast' or 'The Brassbounder'. For indoor games we had ping pong on the big dining-room table or quoits, and for musical entertainment there was the piano which my father and mother occasionally played and the HMV mahogany gramophone which was wound up on special days.

There were about forty records in the collection, including four sides of Harry Lauder [Roaming in the Gloaming, Stop your Tickling, Jock amongst them] and other old favourites such as Silver Threads among the Gold or The Bells of St Malo by the band of the Coldstream Guards. There were a few more recent additions including the famous rendering of

'I know that my re-deemer liveth' by Master E Clough accompanied by G Thalben Ball. I still have the gramophone and the records but what an incongruous concert we would give with them today!

The gramo-phone went into

THE OLD HMV GRAMOPHONE. PHOTO: AUTHOR

virtual retirement when the BBC came on the scene. My father strung an aerial between the house and the granary and put together a crystal set which did duty until battery wireless sets came along, first with separate dry [high tension] and wet [low tension] batteries and then with both LT and HT combined in one. On some winter evenings we would sit round the fire with our earphones on and listen to the farming programme with James Scot-Watson, or perhaps the music hall or the Reverend Dick Shepherd preaching from St Martin in the Field. Then we had a loud speaker set, but television was still some way away.

Our house must, in earlier times, have housed a small retinue of servants in the attics. To help my mother, there was only Mrs Bridges, wife of the foreman on John Larter's adjoining farm, who came over on wash days. She was a small, bustling woman with a family of her own - Freddy, Gerald and Victor (who later came to work at the D'Urbans) and an elder pretty daughter who disappeared from the scene - I can dimly recall that it was said that she was 'in the family way' and I hope the poor disgraced girl had a happy life, wherever it was that she went. My mother also had help, at busy times, from 'nurse'. Nurse Gallant had been midwife at my, and my younger sister's, birth and she continued after retiring from midwifery, to come and stay at the D'Urbans for months at a time. She was a wonderful person to have helping us in the farmhouse in those years.

When the harvest had been gathered in my mother would prepare a harvest supper, with chairs round the big kitchen table for both the regular farm staff and for the part-time men. There would be roast beef and beer; and one of the Smith clan , who had a pleasant baritone, would sing songs such as Buttercup Joe. But who, today, would want to go back to those old, ill-paid, backbreaking routines?

The big pond where the horses drank had an island in it and the waterhens nested there. I had my barque on the pond - an old barn door fixed across two long logs, with a mast stepped amidships and a sacking sail, made from a Kositos bag. Kositos was a form of flaked maize used for pig food and, being light, it needed extra large hessian sacks, so that one sack, split down the side, would make a good mainsail. I couldn't tack or point up into the wind, but that did not prevent me from imagining that I was a hardy seaman before the mast.

4
_____

The Farm Worker

The farm worker's regular weekly wage was thirty shillings {£1.50 in modern money} but Frank Banthorpe, the foreman, earned thirty-two and also had the privilege of keeping a hut full of hens in the Lower Horse Meadow and feeding them with the tail corn from the threshing machine. Even allowing for their rent-free cottages, free firewood and well-kept kitchen gardens, the wages were pitifully small. Requirements and expectations were also small in comparison with modern needs, but it still astonishes me that David Smith, the horseman, had never seen the sea - only 14 miles away at Aldeburgh.

David had known really hard times when his two sons, who now brought two standard wages into the cottage, were still too young to work. It was normal for the men to stop ploughing for 'elevenses' - invariably bread and cheese - but David was reduced to taking a hunk of stale bread instead of the Cheddar which he could not afford. He ate bread and bread instead of bread and cheese, and hoped the others would not see how poor he was. Times were better in the nineteen thirties and he could afford some shag tobacco for his short-stemmed clay pipe and a weekend pint of beer at the Crown and Anchor.

The cheap clay pipes when new had stems several inches long and these stems were brittle and, seemingly, made to be broken. It was remarkable how many short lengths of old pipe stems were turned up in ploughing arable fields - pieces that had snapped off the pipes of generations of smokers, either in the fields or in the farm yards where they found their way into manure which later was spread on the fields. It is unlikely that the broken pieces of old pipe stems are noticed nowadays - tractors travel too fast and their drivers sit in enclosed cabs, too far from the soil to notice such details.

David took Lloyd George's pension at age 70 when I was still a small boy but I can remember enough of him to realise that he was the epitome of Victorian/Edwardian skilled farm workers. He had a wonderful way with horses; he was always in charge of our steerage drill and the lines of corn were immaculately straight.

PULLING YARD MANURE FROM THE CART.
LINE DRAWING BY MARY STANIFORTH.

People today cannot conceive the care that was taken with farm yard manure. Our muck hill was not the sloppy heap of waste material that one now sees, but a square-walled edifice which David had turned and composted. He would then lead the manure out in a horse-drawn tumbril and set it out, with his muck croomb, into identically sized heaps, spaced with geometrical precision. He would not have to lead the horse by hand, but would guide it by means of the three commands - 'Wheesh' or 'go right; 'Coobi' or 'go left' and 'Whoa' for 'stop' - so that he could pull off the manure exactly where he wanted it. Later he would spread the manure with his spring-tined fork with perfect evenness. His work was the foundation of a way of arable farming that had prospered in the golden age but which became completely uneconomic with the exploitation of the prairies.

Socially, men like David Smith, though financially poor, were not mere proletarian labourers. His eldest son Ernest would sometimes enliven the summer evening air with a tune from his melodeon as he sat outside the cottage door. His bachelor brother George made a living from a small pig farm a mile up the road from the D'Urbans: he supplemented this in the later thirties by keeping pigs in the unused stock yards at the D'Urbans and he took on Freddy Bridges when he left school to cope with the increased work. George would walk down to Framlingham once or twice a week and repair to the Conservative Club on Castle Street where he would rub shoulders with other local worthies, including masters from Framlingham College.

David passed on his abilities to his son, Ernest, who succeeded him as our horseman. These included the art of corn stack building. The sheaves, carted in from stooks in the field, had to be firmly arranged in courses up to a height of perhaps eight or ten feet with a pitched roof so made that it could be thatched. The outer courses of sheaves had to be placed tightly together and stamped down to give a firm wall to the stack with the inner courses overlapping to hold all together. It was considered shameful if a stack were seen to bulge so that it had to be shored up.

None of our men and few in the parish would thatch the stacks. This was left to Bob Moore, a specialist, who would

PULLONG WHEAT STRAW FOR THATCHING.

come as soon as he could after harvest to cover the stacks. The thatch itself would be drawn from a wetted heap of last year's threshed wheat straw left over for the purpose. The pulled 'yealms' of straw were laid so that they overlapped and close together. The thatch was then fastened to the roof with binder twine attached to 'broaches' - three-foot-long sharpened pegs of split hazel which were pressed into the roof. Groups of thatched stacks, once such a feature of the landscape in arable areas, are no longer seen, but the art of thatching is, happily, flourishing, though now only for covering buildings.

5

Framlingham in the
Twenties & Thirties

Framlingham had a Saturday market and, as a small boy, I would be sent down to buy fresh Lowestoft herrings from the fish stall. Next door there was often a riveting performer who would eat glass and whose *tour de force* was to swallow a watch, while keeping hold of the end of the chain. We were invited to listen to the ticking of the watch through his singlet.

The town at that time had a small gas works for street lighting and domestic supply, but no piped water or sewage system and no electricity.

At the end of the square, beside the Crown and Anchor public house was Durrants the butcher, with whom the D'Urbans farm had an arrangement which may have gone back to the Victorian era. From time to time David would take a cart-load of straw to the lairage behind the butcher's shop and bring back a load of manure. There was no money involved in the deal and it was at least a mile from the farm to the abattoir. The arrangement would seem ludicrous today, but one has to remember that farm yard manure was the basis of soil fertility in those days. Nothing illustrates the revolution from traditional methods of husbandry more clearly than the fact that the author, as a consultant in the eighties, has been called in to advise large abattoirs on methods of disposing of their straw-based lairage bedding - farmers simply do not want this manure.

To have an abattoir and its lairage (the yard where livestock were kept before slaughter) in the middle of the town would seem grossly unhygienic today. There was a second one, too, in a barn on the edge of the town near a butcher's shop on the Saxtead road. I used to pass this on my way to school and occasionally peeped through a crack in the door to watch in horrified fascination the slaughter man poleaxe a bullock or cut the throat of a shrieking pig.

However, gentility also made its appearance in town around 1930, with the opening of the Condul Cafe in the market square, well away from Durrants the butcher and opposite the entrance to St Michael's Church. It owed its name to the two sisters, Constance and Dulcie, who ran it. My mother would very occasionally take us there for tea and a slice of Swiss roll.

Another important event in the 1930's was the arrival one day of the Michelin team to demonstrate their tyres, The market square was cleared, rain arrived on time, and the drivers, with Gaulloises hanging from their lips, I remember, flung their skidding, squealing cars around, to universal delight. Did it affect sales? I can only say that my family always use the Guides Michelin when touring in Europe and I have Michelin tyres on my present car.

There were several forms of entertainment in the town, including football. Framlingham Town was the main club, but for a year or two we even had another team, Framlingham United, which played on a flat but muddy meadow on Major Rolfe's farm. The Framlingham Amateur Dramatic Society [The FADS] thrived in those days and every winter staged shows in the Assembly Rooms; I can only remember one - it must have been about 1935 that they did Chekhov's Three Sisters.

The Suffolk Show now has a permanent show ground near Ipswich but it was peripatetic in those pre-war years, The nearest it came to Framilngham was, I think, in 1926 and my father took me with him to see it. I can remember only the display of poultry breeds - Minorcas, Wyandottes, Leghorns, Orpingtons, Dorkings, Plymouth Rocks and the rest - and sitting on my father's shoulders to watch the tent pegging. The lancers galloped by, spiking and carrying off the tent pegs, if they aimed well, to the applause of the audience, in a display that is now a part of history.

The 'pictures' came to town in the 1930s and I recall my excitement on seeing The Invisible Man in the unjustly described 'flea pit'. A great pageant was staged in 1930 and the college put on a Shakespeare play every other year within the castle walls. Every summer the sound of cheerful, amplified music was wafted over the parish - the fair with dodgems and roundabouts and all the other fun was paying its annual visit. The public houses and the Conservative Club were the hubs of general social gathering. The Framlingham Weekly News was our regular source of local information.

6

The Farming Routine

Life on the farm ran a regular and usually placid course. On Fridays my father would put on his trilby, polish his black leggings, and bicycle down to the bank to collect money for wages.

A seasonal landmark was the delivery of a barrel of beer which my father tapped in the workshop. It was the signal that Nestling's steam engine and threshing tackle would shortly appear to thresh our corn stacks. Extra labour came in from neighbouring farms for this, and the beer was to ensure that the work went with a swing.

Two men were needed to pitchfork the sheaves from the corn stack on to the threshing drum where another man fed them to the operator who cut the bands and fed the beaters in the threshing drum. Two men built the new stack of threshed straw as it came off the pitcher [elevator], with a third in the 'bully hole' when the stack got high; another was assigned to bag off the grain as it issued from the drum and yet another had to remove the chaff and cavings.

The horse beans were always the last to ripen, which was just as well because their coarse woody stems played havoc with the binder canvases.

THRESHING WHEAT IN THE TWENTIES. MERL.

We had a good crop in 1929 and the required size of stack was under-estimated so that there was no room in the roof of the stack for the last two wagon loads. These had to be drawn into the barn to be threshed by flail. There were still three flails tucked behind the wainscotting in the barn – museum pieces, really, left over from Edwardian times. David, our old horseman, was the only workman who had ever used a flail and he instructed us in the procedure. It must have been one of the last occasions on which threshing was done by flail since the threshing drum took over in the 19th century.

It is remarkable that this method of threshing corn has remained virtually the same over many centuries. The Cyclopedia of Modern Agriculture, dated 1910, says that the flail is 'but little used' and there is no mention of it in modern books on agricultural technology.

For some years we grew an acre or so of mangolds which were stored in the beet house. They had to be trimmed and put through a beet slicer before being mixed with chaff and corn for the horses. The slicer was turned by hand and was heavy work. When my father had to reduce the farm labour force we stopped growing mangolds and the slicer went into what was almost certainly final retirement.

In the barn there were two other pieces of machinery that were relics of a bygone age but which we still occasionally used. The chaff cutter consisted of a large wheel carrying curved cutter blades,and a feed box through which straw was continuously fed and sliced, as it emerged, into short lengths. The wheel was turned by hand and it was

THRESHING BY FLAIL IN MEDIEVAL TIMES.
AN ILLUSTRATION FROM THE LUTTREL PSALTER.
BRITISH MUSEUM.

heavy work, performed only when we ran out of the wheat chaff which was stored in the barn for mixing with the horse rations. The winnowing machine was for cleaning up grain samples which sometimes contained too many light grains or were contaminated with, perhaps, bits of barley awns. It had a large fan and, again, was turned by hand, but the work was not so hard as with the chaff cutter.

Extracting clean grain from a crop has been [and still is in some countries] a most laborious business. In some parts of the East grain is dislodged from the ear by literally threshing hand-held bundles of the crop over a frame. Another system is to drive animals round and round over a layer of the cut crop, after

THRESHING RICE ON AN ISLAND IN THE ESSEQUIBO RIVER, BRITISH GUINA, 1943.

which the straw is raked away and the grain is winnowed from the chaff by throwing it up into the breeze. No breeze – no winnowing. A primitive method in parts of Africa is to simply beat the cut crop on the ground. Now, in many countries, the combine harvester is king and threshes as it devours the crop and delivers the clean corn through elevators into attendant trailers. The drawback is that the straw is dumped on the field, straw which used to be essential for feeding and bedding the livestock that produced the manure to feed the crop.

What an extraordinary transformation it has been since that era of 'honest toil' to the present arable crop systems with huge tractors pulling ploughs with six to ten furrows or more, and machines for spreading herbicides and fertilisers and sowing seeds, and self-propelled combine harvesters with their air-conditioned cabs and radios. Our harvest, with the corn and beans cut by binder and stooked and carted and stacked, needed at least five men, with me when I was old enough, to lead the wagons to and from the harvest field. Stooking [or shocking, as it was called in Suffolk] was hard work, particularly when the sheaves were damp and full of thistles.

The change in methods of weed control was perhaps the greatest advance in farming techniques in the twentieth century. Bastard fallowing, horse-hoeing and hand-hoeing used to consume endless hours of labour and did not always keep the weeds at bay. The arrival of chemical herbicides revolutionised the control of weeds.

'THE ERA OF HONEST TOIL'. WEEDING MR. HUSTLER'S ONIONS, AUBOURN, LINCOLN, ABOUT 1950. ONE MAN, WITH TRACTOR-MOUNTED SPRAYER WOULD SOON DO THIS WORK. AUTHOR.

THE LONG-BOOM SPRAYER TOOK OVER FROM THE HAND HOER.

There was always at least one field of 'summerland' at the D'Urbans. The land was left uncropped so that it could be ploughed or cultivated several times in an effort to kill perennial weeds such as couch grass [Agropyrum repens] or speargrass [Agrostis solonifera] which had underground root systems and could not be killed by normal hoeing. The intention was to bake the ploughed clods in the summer sun so that the rhizomes would dry out and die – and it worked in a hot, dry summer. This fallowing, a system often referred to in the bible, had a long innings in English agriculture, through the Middle Ages to Victorian times, but with the advent of chemical fertilisers and herbicides it became a practice of the past.

Yet, among all the labour-saving advances since those pre-war days, there is perhaps one cause for regret – the passing of the farm horse and its replacement by the soulless tractor. I recall Matchet and Smiler and Duke and Prince and Britain and Diamond enjoying my curry-combing as they stood in the stable eating their meal after a hard day's work. I remember especially Diamond, a black mare with a white blaze on her forehead, gathering her strength to pull a wagon-load of sheaves up Pryke's Hill. She was getting on in years and literally 'died in harness' one day at the end of a furrow in the 10-acre. They said it was a heart attack.

THE MARE, DIAMOND; PAINTED BY R.W. STANIFORTH

The regret is, of course, largely sentimental. When they were working, those horses had to be fed and watered at a very early hour in the morning. Their stable had to be kept clean; fresh bedding had to be added regularly in their yard, and hay, cut in those days from the stack with a heavy hay knife, had to be put in their manger. Then there was the harnessing, and unharnessing, and all for a slow rate of work with a man trudging behind them in a furrow on rough land.

Yet I recall one of the pleasantest tasks on the pre-war farm – horse-raking. The binder usually left some of the crop, cut but unbound, on the fields, sometimes an appreciable proportion of the crop if it was of uneven height or standing badly. These 'rakings' had to be drawn together to be loaded loose on to a wagon for transport to the stackyard. One sat on an iron seat, cushioned with a sack, with the horse in shafts and the reins in your hand. It would be a fine day, with the larks singing, and the art was to pull the trip lever at just the right moment so that the row of rakings was in a tidy, straight swath.

The tractor, when it came, was perhaps unlovely and smelly, but it needed only to be fuelled with paraffin [plus a little petrol for starting in the early models]. Our small Fordson would plough two furrows where a pair of horses would plough only one, and the driver sat on a seat. And the modern big tractor, with its air-conditioned cab and built-in radio, can do the work of several stables of horses.

It is small wonder that official statistics show that the number of horses used for agriculture dropped from almost a million in 1921 to around 20,000 in 1972. The number of tractors increased correspondingly from about 30,000 to around half a million over the same period.

However, it was not until after World War II that the steep decline in farm horse numbers set in. I spent the summer vacation of 1940 on Mr Richard Carley's farm at Badingham; he was a council member of the Suffolk Horse Society and at their Ipswich sale that year good mares made up to 92 guineas and geldings to 80 guineas – high prices at that time. The Society was also trying to introduce new blood into the pedigree breed and farmers who owned horses of the right colour and conformation were invited to have them inspected and, if approved, given provisional entry. Mr Carley carried our several such inspections at the farm when I was there and we did not foresee the virtual elimination of the farm horse that was shortly to occur.

In parenthesis here one should mention the temporary intrusion of steam power during the transition from animal draught to the internal combustion engine. Steam was tried out in several ways*, but we saw only one at the D'Urbans and it was on a neighbouring field of John Larter's in 1929. There were two steam engines stationed at opposite ends of the field and they operated winding gear which dragged a multiple-furrowed reversible plough back and forth. It was effective in a square field but looked laborious. Some manufacturers produced quite light steam tractors which pulled implements in the normal way. However, steam power did not spread widely at this time, and the petroleum-fuelled tractor, wheeled and caterpillar-tracked, took over. At the time of writing, though, there is talk of the possibility of petroleum sources drying up and of new and improved steam systems making a comeback.

Tractors have increased enormously in power since my father bought his little Fordson. They can range in power today from around 30 to 200 horse power and the biggest 4-wheel drive and crawler tractors can cost up to £100,000. Other farm machinery has increased similarly in size and cost and a combine harvester with a cutter bar width of 20 to 25 feet can now cost around £135,000**.

An even more startling comparison would be between the weekly farm worker's pay at the D'Urbans farm of £1.50 for a sixty hour week and the current statutory minimum wage of around £230 for a general farm worker, for a 39-hour week, rising to perhaps £350 with overtime.*

In my mind's eye I see David Smith scraping the clay off his hob-nailed boots on the high step of the stable door after a hard day's ploughing. He could never have dreamed of the farming revolution of the past seventy years.

* See Farm Machinery, 1750-1945, by Jonothan Brown, Batsford, 1989.

** See Farm Management Pocketbook, by John Nix, 34th Edn., 2004. Imperial College, London, Wye Campus.

8

_____

Some Events on the Farm

I was still very small when the Oaks farm house, where my mother and father had started farming, was burned down. I can only dimly remember the horse-drawn Framlingham fire engine galloping up the still untarred road on its way to the blaze. The story of the fire brigade and the way it worked is well told in Muriel Kilvert's book.* At this time, the voluntary firemen had first to be called out by the clangour of the church bells and the horses had to be caught in their field on the Saxmundham road and harnessed to the engine. How news of the Oaks Farm fire, right at the edge of the parish, got to the town I do not know. There was no direct telephone in those days and it may be that a neighbour with a car saw the outbreak and drove with the news into Framlingham.

In any case this outing of the brigade was a hopeless enterprise and the house was burned to the ground. There were dark rumours at the time that Jack Priest had set fire to his house to obtain insurance money. He was reported as saying that the fire had started because he had left his socks in the oven to dry - which did not seem too plausible an explanation. For some years after the fire Mr Priest resided in a calf house among the farm buildings and I can remember peeping in, during one of my bird-nesting sorties, and seeing the rough-made bed and his 12-bore shotgun leaning in the corner.

I have only a dim recollection of the time in the early twenties when meal was brought to the farm by horse and cart from Saxtead windmill, which was still working then. We later got our supplies from a corn merchant in Framlingham. On Saturdays, Charlie Gooch, who was said to have gypsy blood and wore a thin gold ring in his ear, would come, again with horse and cart, with these supplies. The bags of meal were easy and I could carry them in, but the maize in 18-stone sacks was heavy. Yet it was normal in those days to carry these back-breaking loads of grain on a man's back, even up a steep flight of granary stairs. A man's usefulness for farm work depended, in local lore, on his ability to 'carry corn'.

One day, Frank Banthorpe appeared at our back door, looking worried and asked to see my father. The two of them went off and came back a little later with the news that Charlie Gooch had drowned himself in the pond between the two horse meadows. Why he had walked out all the way from Framlingham, wandered up the Soham Lane and across several fields to drown himself in that pond we could not tell. Someone said that he had had much trouble with his teeth and that his encounters with the dentist had upset him. This I could understand. The only dental practitioner in Framlingham at that time was an unqualified man who came once a week to a small room near Barclays Bank; I well remember his excruciating drill, operated by a foot pedal.

A year or two later there occurred another event that sticks in my memory. At weekends I used to take Lassie, our wire-haired fox terrier, for a walk round the farm; she loved to chase rabbits but rarely caught one. We were in Stonelands when we heard a far-off cry for help. We made for the sound, across three fields and, on the farm boundary, came across Mr Brown, the Kettleborough farmer, wedged in a ditch and unable to get out - he was afflicted with dropsy. I managed to haul him out and get him back to his house.

He would often be chauffeured in to Framlingham in one of those early, high-backed Citroens for a visit to the Conservative Club and a shave from Sonny Moore, the town barber in Castle Street. I had my hair cut there - at three pence a time - and, while I waited my turn, enjoyed watching an artist at work with his lather and cut-throat. Incidentally, my father must have been one of the early users of a Gillette safety razor and I never knew him go to the barber.

However, he had his opinion of proper form and was indignant when Mr Brown, the morning after his escape from a possibly sticky end, had his car stopped when he saw me sharpening knives on the binder cutter bar beside the road in Nettus Arms and presented me with a florin. My father insisted that I give it back. No hard feelings resulted and Mr Brown often lent me his two-speed bicycle. He always wore spats on his visits to the town - the last man I ever knew to sport these emblems of bourgeois status.

When Victor, Mrs Bridges' youngest son, reached the age of fourteen he, like most youngsters at that time, left Hitcham's School and, he came, by long-standing arrangement, to work for my father. One of his first summer jobs was to bring the horses in from their grazing, first thing in the morning, and he decided one day, very recklessly, to take a ride on one of them when he rounded them up, at some distance from the farm, in the lower horse meadow. It was, of course, a bareback ride and he fell off the big, 16-hands horse and broke his leg. It was a simple fracture and was soon set in plaster but he was off work for a few weeks – I cannot recall exactly for how long but I am sure my father paid his small wage for that time. No-one thought of litigation and legal compensation in those days.

9
_____

Rabbits & Other Pests

The bunnies were not exactly our furry friends. Those who romanticise rabbits conveniently forget that they breed six times a year (or more) with litters of six (or more), that they laid waste to vast areas of Australia after their introduction to that continent, before myxomatosis came to the Australians' relief, and that they have caused untold damage to forestry and farming over many years in this country. At the D'Urbans they would graze growing wheat and barley and we could ill afford the loss of crop.

In its section on rabbits, the Standard Cyclopedia of Modern Agriculture [Gresham, 1910] says, 'In an evil hour for our colonists they were introduced into Australia during the 19th century, and have increased there beyond all control, doing incalculable damage to crops and pasture. In such hordes do they move in Victoria that the very dogs that were intended to keep them in check refuse to look at them.' It goes on to say that, 'The only way in which the presence of rabbits should be tolerated in a civilised and highly cultivated country is to enclose spaces of waste or other land as warrens .... In Mr Lloyd Price's warren at Rhiwlas in Carnarvonshire, on 5th October 1885, a party of nine guns shot 5106 rabbits in seven hours'.

At the D'Urbans there were many burrows along the Gull and also a small warren at the far end of Stonelands, as well as odd rabbit burrows in ditch sides. There was always some rabbit grazing and in badly attacked fields half the crop would commonly be lost. However, even before the arrival of myxomatosis, the population seemed to vary from year to year, perhaps because of some disease or extra severe predation by stoats or cats.

We had stoats on the farm though we seldom saw them. However, I once saw a stoat confronting a rabbit in the Lower Horse Meadow. The rabbit was completely petrified and paralysed with fear but managed a terrified squeal as the stoat dispatched it.

Charlie Wright, an antique dealer in the town, who used to come from time to time to tune our piano, had, I suppose as *quid pro quo*, an open invitation to shoot rabbits in the Gull, but he did not kill many. In those days the cruel gin trap had not been outlawed and I have to admit that, as a boy, I became adept at setting these traps in the sandy entrances to the burrows and caught a good many in that way.

Another way of trying to reduce the rabbit menace was ferretting. Rabbits are terrified of ferrets, as they are of their cousins, stoats. By letting ferrets into their burrows they can be made to bolt into nets. But the procedure is not straightforward and you always have to bring a good spade when you go ferretting. The ferrets, normally tethered to a line, can become entangled underground, particularly if there are roots in the warren. The only time I ever went ferretting we spent most of the time digging out a lost ferret. The difficulty can now be overcome by attaching sonar to the ferret's neck so that its whereabouts can be followed from above ground.

A more exciting attack on the rabbits was at harvest time. Imagine the scene as the binder gradually reduced the area of rabbit-infested corn until it was, perhaps no more than six yards wide. A few wise rabbits would have escaped while the going was safer, but now the rest were hemmed in, with 50 yards or more of open stubble to cross before they could reach safety in their burrows. A bunch of local lads would be there with heavy sticks while Gerald patrolled the diminished plot of standing corn with his catapult and pocket full of pebbles. Now and then he would spot a rabbit lying crouched in a weedy patch of corn and he was deadly with his elastic-powered missiles, My father would stand at one corner with his 12-bore and he was a good shot, too, when the rabbits broke cover. We boys would chase escaping rabbits with sticks; some would reach safety, others would be struck down and some would hide under sheaves. The trick was to fling oneself over the sheaf where you thought the animal was hiding and grab it with one hand, hold it up by its back legs and dispatch it with a karate chop behind the ears

A word about catapults. These dangerous weapons were much prized by country lads at that time and they could be bought, ready-made, with metal forks, in shops in the town, if you could afford them. However, we had little money and it was much cheaper to mark down a young ash, with branches sprouting opposite each other on the stem, cut out the central shoot, and train the two branches so that they formed a natural fork. After a year or so the stem and branches would be strong enough to be cut to size, making a perfect 'crotch' on which to fit the elastic bands and missile pouch. The bands, about a quarter of an inch square in section, and of suitable length, could be bought cheaply in more than one shop and the pouch could be made from the tongue of an old shoe. This is a rural craft which, happily, has declined and it would be hard to find either the catapults themselves or the parts from which they could be made in country shops.

When the binder had finished its work, the rabbits, perhaps 30 or 40 of them from a badly infested field, would be heaped on the binder's platform canvas and distributed to the hunters. Young ones were the best - there is nothing more tasty than a well-fried three-quarters grown wild rabbit.

There were other, less tasty, pests on the farm. Rooks could thin out germinating crops but we had no nearby rookery or roost and a good scarecrow usually kept them away. It was not till I worked for MAFF in Lincolnshire that that I saw serious damage from these birds on a farm in Swinderby parish. At that time the ministry required the NAAS and the Agricultural Executive Committees to encourage rook shooting and the Swinderby farmer and I shot a number of young rooks as they left the nests. Next day I was invited to partake of rook pie at the farm, but it was not very tasty. Perhaps his mother's recipe was not the best and did not follow the instructions given in Farmhouse Fare, Farmers Weekly, 1944, which included the following:

SOMERSET ROOK PIE WITH FIGGY PASTRY

6 rooks
Pieces of fat bacon cut in chunks.
Weak stock Pepper and salt to taste.

For the paste.
1 lb of flour 4 ozs raisins stoned.
Half lb. fat Pepper and salt to taste.
4 ozs. currants.

Bake the rooks, which must have been skinned; using only the legs and breast, as all other parts are bitter. They should be left soaking in salt and water overnight. In the morning, drain away the brine and put the legs and breast in a good-sized pie dish, adding the fat bacon. Cover with the stock, and season well with pepper and salt.

PASTRY. Rub the fat well into the flour, adding pepper and salt, then add the currants and raisins. Mix well and add sufficient water to make a stiff paste. Roll out to about three quarters of an inch thick, then place right over the pie, letting it come right over the sides. Cover the pie with a piece of greaseproof paper, and then put the pudding cloth on top. Tie well down and see that the water has no chance of getting in. There must be sufficient water in your boiler to cover it. Do not put the pie in until the water is boiling. The pie takes a good 3 hours to cook, and is delicious served with gooseberry jelly.

From Miss G. M. Dinham, Wiltshire.

I wonder how many readers of Farmhouse Fare actually tried this recipe of wartime Britain, when meat was scarce. I guess that few would attempt it now, in this age of packaged food.

Wood pigeons severely damaged clover crops in some years - flocks of them descending on the fields, eating the hearts out of the plants. We would shoot them from a field-side hide, using decoys. They made rather better eating than rooks and there are attractive recipes in Farmhouse Fare.

Mice sometimes got into corn stacks and bred there. The destruction wrought by a bad infestation, perhaps seen only when the stack was opened for threshing, could be devastating. I remember one such stack, with its sheaves chewed to pieces and the mice jumping out as they lost their shelter. We surrounded the stack with wire netting and our terrier must have killed scores of them. Mice are not found in the British diet, but my son on V S O work in Nyasaland [now Malawi] found that they were considered good to eat in that country.

Wasps were another pest in some years and my father kept a bottle of potassium cyanide in a safe place and would stuff cotton wool soaked with the poison in the entrance to the wasps' nest, in the evening when they had returned home. This invariably exterminated the swarm. I have never heard of wasps being eaten anywhere but, in Africa, insects such as termites, locusts and shield bugs, are eaten with relish in some areas and bees are said to be eaten in Brazil.

10

Birds & Egg Collecting

It is curious that my interest in birds and egg collection was stimulated by two clergymen. I have aleady mentioned the Methodist church in Framlingham, and the minister, the Reverend Bywater, had a consuming interest in bird photography. He would come out to our farm and I would

tell him where there were birds nesting. He took some good pictures of blue tits that nested in our Beauty of Bath apple tree and of nesting wrens. We went once to one of the surviving great oaks in which an owl was nesting and he took the photo-graph shown left.

YOUNG OWLETS: A PHOTOGRAPH IN
REMEMBRANCE OF THE REVEREND BYWATER.

Mr Bywater had a young family and was sadly drowned when sea bathing one summer at Thorpeness. What would he have thought of an apparatus made and patented by my son which consists of a tiny infrared camera set above a blue tit's (or other) nest and which transmits the moving picture to ones television screen?

I have to admit that I collected birds' eggs. My father impressed on me that I must not disturb nests or take more than one egg and I still do not consider that I deserved to be branded a wild life vandal, as I would be by a modern ecologist. Rarely if ever did a bird desert its nest because of my attentions. I eventually had about a hundred different eggs in my collection and I can only commiserate with those who have never seen the heavenly blue of a dunnock's egg or the romantic olive of a nightingale's.

Why should a drab little dunnock's egg be so beautiful? It is laid and then just sat upon by a parent bird till it hatches after which the shell is tipped unceremoniously out of the nest. It is hard to find a Darwinian explanation. Some eggs, such as the mottled and spotted brown eggs of the lapwing, are camouflaged to make them difficult to spot in their shallow nest scratched in the soil. Others, like martins', owls or kingfishers', are laid in dark holes and are plain white - a sensible economy of pigment. But why the cerulean blue of the dunnock's egg, or for that matter the pretty, speckled robin's or blue tit's eggs which are laid in dark. covered nests?

Most of the eggs I found on our own farm but some were from other, sometimes inaccessible, places. I had to climb the walls of Framlingham castle for my jackdaw's egg and my rook's egg was from the rookery at neighboring Kettleburgh rectory. There was a nest there that I thought was reachable. It meant throwing a long length of weighted binder twine over a high branch of a Scots pine and pulling up an attached stout plough trace that I borrowed from the stable. I climbed up the rope, reached over to the nest, popped one of the five eggs into my mouth and abseiled down to terra firma. If my mother had known of this dangerous escapade I am sure she would have been horrified.

I knew some heronries, too, but in those the birds nested right at the top of very tall trees. I never came across a nest that I could climb to, even with the aid of a plough trace, and no heron's egg ever found its way into my collection.

Predators did much more damage than I ever did. My nightingale's egg came from a thick hawthorn bush in the Gull and I later found that the four remaining eggs had been broken up, perhaps by a magpie or more probably by a jay that had a nest nearby. Magpies were not common in those days, with every gamekeeper's hand against them, since they took partridges' and pheasants' eggs.

My guide in the quest for eggs was a small volume published in 1862 by Routledge, Warne & Routledge, entitled 'British Birds, Eggs and Nests, popularly described by the Reverend J C Atkinson, with illustrations by W S Coleman.'

This handbook is based on many years' observations by the Victorian vicar and is directed to 'the youthful nest hunter and egg collector'. It has much to say about the birds themselves and their habits and songs, as well as about their nests an eggs. Something of the flavour of the text comes over in a passage about a hawk - 'if you hear some careful, Martha-like, housewife of a hen, skirling and fussing, in dire alarm, her terrified chicks the while, seeking any possible shelter, you may be almost certain that the gliding form you caught a glimpse of rounding the corner of the barn and making a rapid, but by no means noisy stoop, among the young poultry of various kinds in lively attendance on their mothers, you may be tolerably sure that the intruder was a Sparrow Hawk, and that some hapless dove or chicken has lost the number of his mess'. This long out of print book is a charming period piece of information.

The illustrations, given the limitations of Victorian reproduction, have kept their colours well and they helped me to distinguish between, say, a linnet's and a skylark's egg.

The Reverend Atkinson acknowledges one of the misgivings about egg collecting that has come to prominence in recent years. 'The author', he writes, ' has been gravely taken to task by some of his conscientious friends for delineating .... the pleasures and excitements of egg hunting ....He has been more than once asked - Do you really mean to encourage boys in robbing birds' nests? If I thought there was any real or necessary connection between a love of egg hunting .... and cruelty, I would not say another word for it or about it'. He goes on to compare the careful taking of an egg 'by the true lover of birds and their ways and their nests and eggs, which causes so far as human observation can reach .... no concern to the little owners', with the destruction of nests and their surroundings 'by some loutish country savages'.

Legislation has now been passed, more than a century after that country parson's time, making it a criminal offence to collect birds' eggs. This is an understandable reaction to the shameless stealing of some rare birds' eggs for financial gain. This legislation is justified but it can appear draconian to the old breed of amateur bird lovers and egg collectors - of whom there are not in any case a great many. I used to include a question about the colour of birds' eggs in the quiz competitions that I ran for Young Farmers Clubs and it was always surprising how few of these country people had any knowledge of birds' eggs - and this was long before the law against collecting.

As with many of Nature's wonders, one had to marvel at the variety in the construction of the nests themselves. Just a few crossed twigs for the turtle dove - you could see the eggs from underneath - to the elaborate, well-lined domed structures of the long-tailed tit. The parson, too, wondered at the different ways in which birds build their nests and his comment is from the scriptures. 'O Lord how manifold are thy works! In wisdom hast thou made them all!'

11

Rays of Encouragement

During the inter-war period the government took some steps to alleviate the distress among arable farmers.

One was the introduction in the Wheat Act of 1936 of the wheat quota system. Under this there was provision for a deficiency payment for millable wheat sold by registered growers. The deficiency was the difference between the fixed standard price and the 'ascertained average' price paid by millers on the free market. The scheme ensured that consumers' interests were safeguarded while, at the same time, the grower was encouraged to make the best price possible for his individual output of millable grain, in the knowledge that he, in common with all the other registered growers, would receive identical deficiency payments per ton sold. The Quota had the effect of putting a floor under the farmer's price – but this floor, set at about £10 per ton, was extremely low. As can be imagined, the ascertainment of the average price paid in a scattered market along with the registration of growers and the recording of their sales of millable grain, was a formidable administrative task and the final payment to farmers was often slow in arriving.

Another measure – the Sugar Beet Act of 1925 – had provided for the setting up of beet processing factories in arable areas to which farmers were encouraged to supply beet. Severe shortage of sugar in the first world war, and the fear that some future blockade would reduce supplies from our traditional sources in the West Indies, was behind the move. European countries, notably Germany, had produced sugar from beet for many years.

Under the new British scheme, farmers agreed acreage contracts with their local factory and supplied beet on the basis of permits over the harvesting season. The loads of beet were weighed on arrival at the factory, and sampled for excessive tops and for dirt content – 'tare' – and the samples were analysed for sugar content. Payment was made at once by post to the farmer and these regular cheques throughout the pulling season were a real boost to morale at this time. At first there were some questions as to how representative were the samples taken at the factory. Had some soil from the bottom of the lorry been added, to increase the proportion of 'tare'? The difficulty was overcome by appointing farmers' representatives to be present at the time the samples were taken.

The guaranteed regular income from the beet was a great attraction, but it was obtained at a price in hard labour that would seem unthinkable today. In the first place, fine seed beds for sowing the beet were difficult to obtain on our heavy soil and depended greatly on whether there had been hard winter frost to break down the ploughed land. There had to be good germination and a high plant population for satisfactory beet yields. The plants had to be hoed to keep them free from weeds and 'chopped out' and singled to give the required spacing between plants. Singling was difficult because the beet seed at that time contained up to three 'germs' which germinated closely together so that the hoer had to bend to the work and often had to pull out superfluous plants by hand. All this careful hoeing was backbreaking work, much of it by casual labour, including myself in school holidays. In the muddy conditions men wore strips of sacking round their legs, tied on with binder twine. But worse was to come.

The lifting of the beet had been done individually, using a long narrow spade, in some continental countries, but our system was to loosen the roots with a type of horse-drawn mole plough, after which the beet were pulled by hand, knocked together to shake off as much adhering soil as possible and laid in neat rows. The next step was to go down the rows with a special beet hook, picking up each beet with the hook at the end of the blade, topping them accurately and throwing the topped beet into heaps from which they were forked into tumbrils and taken to roadside clamps. Then the beet had to be forked into lorries to be taken to the factory. All this was truly backbreaking work and was particularly unpleasant one year in the Christmas school holiday when I gave a hand with a late crop in frosty weather.

There was a small bonus to all this, The tops left on the land provided useful sheep keep and a neighbouring farmer used to fold his flock on our tops at, I seem to remember, a nominal six old pence per acre. The treading of the sheep and their dung were good for the next crop which was usually spring barley.

Today, with monogerm seed and precision drills it is so much easier to get good plant populations and spacing. There are now selective herbicides to take care of the weeds; and the modern beet harvesters can lift. clean and elevate direct into trailers at a fraction of the cost in labour that we had to expend before the war at the D'Urbans farm.

There were some other government moves before World War II designed to improve agricultural production. The Agriculture Act of 1937 provided for subsidies to reduce the cost of lime to farmers by 50 per cent and of basic slag [a phosphatic fertiliser] by 25 per cent. This Act also provided for grants of up to 50 per cent for minor arterial and farm drainage. The land at the D'Urbans was not acid, so that the lime subsidy did not affect us; and our ditches had always been maintained so that the drainage grants were of little benefit to us. I did not see the great effect that these grants had in other districts until I worked for MAFF after the war.

12

Science to the Rescue

Every autumn my father would buy a number of square brown paper packets of 'blue stone' - crystals of copper sulphate. This was one of the earliest of the chemicals to be widely used to combat plant diseases.

The condition in question was stinking smut, or bunt - an unpleasant disease of the wheat crop which destroyed ears of corn and left spores which smelt of fish and blew on to the developed grain of other ears. A solution of copper sulphate in water was mixed on the barn floor with the seed wheat for the following crop. It gave good control of the bunt and was the forerunner of a host of seed treatments that were introduced after the war.

During the years of depression in the twenties and thirties the agricultural industry was forced to look for scientific aids to reduce production costs. Some of the most far-reaching advances were in poultry production and we at the D'Urbans farm took part, step by step, in that revolution in the poultry industry - or 'chicken farming' as it used, disparagingly, to be called.

When I was very small we had a farm flock of about forty hens living in the hen house attached to the barn. They were a mixture of Rhode Island Reds, Plymouth Rocks and White Wyandotts and they roamed around the farmyard -- truly free range birds. They probably laid about forty eggs per bird per annum, with those that lived to a ripe old age of four or five laying many fewer than the younger birds. They laid mostly in nest boxes in the hen house, but sometimes in nests around the yard, a favourite place being under the manger in the horse yard. If I was lucky and found a nest I was given a penny. These stray eggs had, of course, to be put in a bucket of water-- if they floated they were addled. The hens laid nearly all their eggs in spring and summer providing enough for the family needs, with a few for sale, and the rest were preserved in a solution of isinglass. This sealed the eggshells but the preserved eggs never tasted as good as new-laid.

After harvest our little flock was put into portable huts and wheeled into stubble fields where they gleaned the grain lost in bindering, stooking and carting. One of my earliest recollections is of going out with my father at dusk to shut the pop holes in these huts so that a fox could not get at them. (Anyone who as seen the carnage wrought by a fox in a

POULTRY OUT ON FREE RANGE. PHOTO: MERL

hen house has little sympathy for Reynard). It would be getting dark as we walked home and I remember my father pointing out the Plough and the North Star and the Seven Sisters, six of them easily visible but the seventh hard to discern. She is Merope, wife of Sisyphus, who, according to Greek mythology, hid her face in shame at having married a mortal. Most of the astronomy I ever knew I gained from those evening walks.

It should be said here, however, that life was not all rosy for the old barnyard flock. Aside from predation by foxes and hawks, the birds could suffer from various parasites, internal as well as external. Among the latter were the mites that caused scaly leg and other unpleasant afflictions. We countered them with pesticides which included the piratical-sounding Black Leaf 40, based on nicotine.

With the cereal crops losing money my father decided to try his luck with a poultry enterprise -- it would be called diversification in the modern jargon. The farmyard flock was moved into huts in the meadow in pens surrounded by chicken wire and he began to concentrate on pure-bred Rhode Island Reds [R I R] which were considered the best layers of fine brown eggs. It was the end of true free range, but they had the run of their pens, being prevented from flying over the wire by having their wings clipped. It was the first move toward the environmentalists' anathema -- intensification.

My father bought a couple of pedigree R I R cockerels to go with the hens and built a range of nest boxes in an outhouse where broody hens were brought in to sit on clutches of eggs. Broodiness did not always coincide with an accumulation of hatching eggs and he used, if necessary, to deceive the newly broody hen by giving her china eggs to sit on -- otherwise she would have lost the mood to sit and would have gone into a moult. The sitting hens had to be taken off the eggs daily for feeding and, after the three week incubation period, produced their happy little broods of chicks and were transferred with them to hen coops on our lawn. It was a system to warm the heart of animal rights enthusiasts, but it obviously was far too laborious to provide the larger laying flocks that everyone could see were needed.

So we started with incubators, at first of 100 egg capacity. With these the only hand labour required daily was for turning the eggs -- an operation which the sitting hen did naturally. Almost as soon as the incubators came into general use, a scourge known as bacillary white diarrhoea (BWD) hit the poultry industry. This disease is as nasty as it sounds and afflicts the newly hatched chicks with generally fatal results. BWD was a disaster and something had to be done. Fortunately, the Americans discovered that it was inherited and that the hens that carried BWD could be detected by a test. You took a sample of the hens blood from inside her wing and mixed it with the Lee antigen; if it coagulated you did not breed from that hen. (Older birds could be infected without showing obvious signs of the disease). The Suffolk Egg and Poultry Producers Association [SAPPA], which my father joined, [and which is still in business] provided a testing service and, by breeding only from uninfected hens, we were able to beat this scourge.

If we knew the source of the bacillus that caused BWD we paid no attention to it. It was none other than *Salmonella pullorum*, (as described in the Ministry of Agriculture leaflet 168), the destroyer introduced to the British public in 1989 by Edwina Currie, Minister for Food in the Conservative Government, causing a scare which all but destroyed our poultry industry. We on the farm had been exposed to the potentially lethal bacillus for many years without suffering the discomfort and even death threatened by Ms Currie. Presumably we had built up an immunity to such diseases by the almost continuous contact we had with them.

We seemed to have good hatching results from the incubator and there would be perhaps ninety fluffy little chicks from 100 eggs. They had to be transferred quickly to wire-floored brooders with canopies, warmed by small Putnam paraffin lamps, under which they huddled to keep warm after they had eaten their chick feed and used the special drinkers. The little things knew nothing of fussing, clucking, mothers and they were next moved into unheated brooders before going out to pens in the meadow.

For egg production, pullets were needed, and the fifty per cent of male chicks in the hatch, from a laying breed like the R I R were were not needed. The trouble was that it was difficult to distinguish male from female for a few weeks, during which they had to be fed and after which their characteristic feathering appeared. One solution suggested at the time was to hire Japanese experts who were reputedly able to 'sex' day old chicks by visual examination. This was an expensive and unsatisfactory solution but poultry geneticists then found a method of cross breeding which enabled pullets to be distinguished from male chicks by means of colour immediately on hatching. They were known as sex- linked breeds.

The next step at the D'Urbans was to give up hatching altogether. It was a time-consuming business and could now be side-stepped by buying day-old chicks from specialist breeders who used very large incubators and mechanised methods. We got our day-old chicks in boxes, usually through SAPPA, and it was amazing how the little things stood the transport and lack of food and drink for perhaps 24 hours. They were always perky on arrival and started to drink immediately in their brooder. It was another step towards 'unnatural' poultry husbandry that seemed to us at the time to be a very logical move, but we did not foresee that incubators would increase in size until they were as big as rooms and hatched tens of thousands of chicks at a time.

Old-fashioned flocks had the great drawback, as mentioned above, of their seasonality of egg production, which was influenced by day length. Eggs tended to be plentiful and cheap in spring and sum-

EARLY BATTERY CAGES. MAFF.

mer and scarce and dear in autumn and winter. Electric light and indoor housing were seen to be the answer to this problem. This was the point at which truly intensive egg production came logically upon the scene. At the D'Urbans we never had more than about 500 layers, with only a few of them in cages.

At that time Sainsbury's was still quite a small firm, but they had an egg collection depot in Framlingham and a van, driven by another

Banthorpe brother, came once a week for our eggs which were packed in standard boxes. The eggs had to be graded for size - they did not want double-yolked or small eggs - and they had to be clean and without the slightest crack. It was often my job to collect the eggs from the nest boxes in the various hen houses and there would always be some dirty ones, particularly in wet weather when the hens picked up dirt in their pens.

So one of the family chores every evening was to go through a couple of bucketfuls of eggs, picking out the ones with dirty spots which had to be wiped clean. If you have ever had to do this sort of work you would appreciate how different it is today , with the hens' eggs rolling down the battery floors, perfectly clean and ready for packing.

The war came, with its tight restriction on poultry feed, but, as soon as it was over, the great revolution in poultry farming resumed at speed. The free-range flock of 40 gave way to the huge, factory farmed flocks of thousands in their batteries to which food and water were automatically conveyed and from which the droppings and eggs were mechanically removed.

The transformation of a branch of farming, which poultry keeping was in my father's day, into a distasteful form of factory production, with caged flocks in their tens of thousands, and 'broilers' on deep litter in units of 100 thousand birds or more, was largely an outcome of the advantages of scale. But it was also encouraged by our system of taxation, as explained by Richard Body in, Our Food, Our Land, Rider, 1991.

When we kept our flock in hen houses in the meadow, we always locked the doors at night and we never had any birds stolen. But others did. There was the case in a neighbouring parish, when a hut full of hens were taken, with a note left pinned to the door, in capital letters reading, 'WE ROB THE RICH TO FEED THE POOR. WE'VE LEFT YOU ONE TO HATCH OUT MORE'.

But we did have a problem with the birds in the meadow when we tried giving them their dry mash from self-feed hoppers. The rats came in hordes to the hoppers and my father shot scores of them, but we had to give up in the end and revert to daily hand feeding, with all the extra labour.

One final comment needs to be made on the revolutionary change that we saw at the D'Urbans from free-range flocks to battery production. Eggs were commonly sold off the farm in the 20s and 30s for around three shillings a dozen (or fifteen present-day pence}. Taking account of inflation, this would now amount to about £4.50. In winter, today, the consumer can buy eggs in the supermarket at £1.40 per dozen, an extraordinary reduction which has been made possible by the application of science to poultry production and the take-over by 'factory farming'. How many of the general public would want producers to go back to the old free range flocks and rearing methods if it meant a tripling of the price of eggs in the shop?

13

Working for MAFF During the War

With the onset of war British farming once more became important. The languishing industry had to be galvanised into activity to feed a country menaced by U-boats. As an agricultural student, I was roped in, during vacation time, by the newly formed Somerset War Agricultural Committee, first to carry out the farm survey and then to operate some of the War Ag's machinery. For the survey I would set out in my uncle's Austin 7 armed with forms supplied by the Taunton office. At the beginning of the survey I used forms designed in the county office, but these were later replaced by the national 'doomsday' survey forms as shown in Appendix I.

A form had to be completed for each farm in every parish in the county and every field had to be outlined in colour on 6-inch Ordnance Survey maps according to the occupier. The standard fee for this work was sixpence per acre and I found that I was landed with leftover parishes and very small farms with often scattered fields - the parishes with bigger, compact farms with big fields having already been surveyed by farmer

members of the committee. Compton-Dundon, my first parish, for instance, was a parish of some 40 farms with an average acreage of around
40, scattered in four or five fields which the owners had acquired when
Lord Ilchester's estate had been broken up and sold to pay death duties.

In a *volte-face* from the general disinterest in farming between the wars,
it was now government policy to scrutinise every individual farm in the
country with a view to increasing output. Farmers rated 'C' under 'management' were in many counties 'put under supervision' or even evicted to
make way for more energetic managers.

Pest officers were appointed to organise control of infestations and
people like myself were employed, while completing the surveys, to discover and schedule land suitable for ploughing. Drainage officers were
brought in to execute plans for clearing the many miles of clogged ditches,
to open up the blocked outfalls of drainage systems which had been installed in more prosperous times and to instal new under drainage where
it was needed. Theodolites and dumpy levels were seen again in the land,
controlling the gradients of tile drainage.

The state of farming had fallen so low that there was no question of
a magic wand quickly transforming the countryside into a well farmed
domain, and the renovation was still in progress when I returned to the
scene after the war. Farmers were still being evicted after 1945, causing
great and lasting resentment.

An article in the Independent newspaper, dated 21st February 2001,
reported that a 'Mr Jim Adams and other farmers who were evicted are
joining forces to appeal for compensation under new European legislation'. Farmers graded 'C' had been made 'to feel like pariahs in their com-
munities, although some War Ags took their roles more seriously than
others'. The extraordinary case of a certain George Walden is quoted in
this article. 'When he refused to leave, police dropped gas bombs down his
chimney. But he had his gas mask and refused to move. In the end, they
came back armed, and he came down, opening fire. The coroner's report
described it as "justifiable homicide".' Such were the lengths resorted to
by the government of the day in pursuit of greater agricultural output.

As can be seen from the survey forms, one of the tasks was to schedule
land for ploughing up. There was a grant of £2 per acre for this but many of
the farmers had little or no cultivation machinery. The War Ag itself had

to organise machinery depots to do the work and I spent all of one summer vacation, with a Fordson tractor and two-furrow Ransome plough, living in an old road-mender's caravan, ploughing up neglected grassland. Returning today to see some of this land, so tidily farmed, it is difficult to recall how scruffy it was, often covered with small bushes and anthills and surrounded by overgrown hedges. The ant hills, or 'emmet humps' as they were called in the Somerset dialect, were sometimes so large and numerous that they had to be laboriously dug out and spread with a spade.

MY CARAVAN IN THE SHADOW OF GLASTONBURY TOR.
AUTHOR'S SKETCH.

To plough this old, run-down grassland so that it could be cultivated to form a good seed bed for the following crop was not a simple task, and the skills of ploughing had been largely lost in the West of England during the farming depression. We ploughmen had to be instructed in the setting of shares and the use of skimmers. The latter were small shares so placed at the front of the plough that they trimmed off the old herbage and turned it into the bottom of the preceding furrow. Without their use, the old grass and weeds would show between the furrows, and grow on in the new crop. Even after rolling and much harrowing, the seedbeds obtained immediately after the old grass tended to be puffy and uneven. The old grass, too, was often full of wire worms for which there was then no chemical cure, and the following crop - usually wheat - was often thin and patchy and low yielding at a time when we needed all the wheat we could grow.

I spent another vacation at Cannington Farm Institute working a thatch-making machine. The art of stack thatching had all but died out in Somerset during the depression years and we had to supply rolls of stitched-together wheat straw to be pegged on the roof of the corn stacks which were now reappearing as a result of the ploughing up campaign.

USING A THATCH-MAKING MACHINE. PHOTO: AUTHOR.

14

Education 🌾

Framlingham had two eighteenth century benefactors, Sir Robert Hit-cham and Sir John Mills. They built almshouses to be occupied by the old and needy and both built and endowed schools for the education of the young. One of the latter was Hitcham's Elementary School where I started formal education and the other was Mills' Grammar School for girls which my three sisters attended.

I began in the infants' section, where we still used slates, and where my earlier lessons at home with Miss Button, the daughter of the farmer at Ivy Farm, Kettleburgh, gave me an advantage. When I moved to the senior part of the school , we got a good grounding in the three Rs as well as some religious instruction once a week from Canon Lanchester and some mild social training. We learned something of the bible from the vicar but I have to admit that the only clear message that I have retained from his lessons is that 'ducks go down for divers reasons and come up for sundry'. I remember, too, that I got special commendation when in the second form, for my artistic lettering and layout of the injunction that CLEANLINESS IS NEXT TO GODLINESS

A sad incident that has stayed in my memory was the death of little Tommy Rose who was knocked down and killed, as he ran across the road to the school, by a van which came, I strangely remember, from Tannington. His small body was carried in and lay under an overcoat in the dark cloakroom until, I suppose, an ambulance came.

Little Tommy's death was one of many such fatalities at that time. It is strange that, in these days when a figure of 2,500 road deaths annually is rightly considered appalling, that there was much greater slaughter on the roads seventy years ago, when traffic was so much lighter. In the five years up to 1934 the annual death toll from car accidents averaged 7000. The carnage in some towns was so great that parents went on strike, refusing to allow their children to go to school until pedestrian bridges or some other form of road crossing had been provided, [Yesterday's Britain, Readers Digest,1998]. There were no traffic lights, zebra crossings, Belisha beacons, lollypop ladies or 30-mile- an-hour speed limits in those days.

There was a playground behind Hitcham's School but no school games such as football or cricket. There was a favourite pastime, however, known as 'Fag Cards'., played in the following manner. You put a cigarette card between the first and second fingers and, with a flick of the wrist, from a kneeling position, propelled it perhaps six or eight feet. Your competitor, or competitors, did likewise, with the aim of landing his card on yours, whereupon the successful player claimed both for his pack. If you missed, as was most likely until there were several cards on the ground, you continued to flick your cards until you landed on another, enabling you to gather in all the cards on the ground. A variety of this game was to set one card upright in a little pile of sand and then to flick your cards so as to knock it flat. Again, the successful flicker took all the cards on the ground. For best results in this variation you would use De Reszke cards; they were thick and stiff and bore photographs of beauty spots such as Watersmeet, whereas lesser breeds of cigarettes, such as Wills or Players, had comparatively lightweight cards with pictures of footballers or flowers.

It seems hardly likely that Fag Cards was a game played only on the playground of Hitcham's School, and it is just recently that I have heard of its existence elsewhere in England. It must surely have been widespread but never seemed to feature alongside, say, shove halfpenny or hop-scotch in handbooks of pastimes. 'Fag Cards' unfortunately had the consequence that the cards became soiled and less suitable for collection into packs.

I did not stay long at Hitcham's as, along with several others, I passed the entrance exam for Framlingham College and started school there as a day-boy, my home being only a mile away.

The Albert Memorial College in the depressed 1930s was short of pupils, and the total of boarders was only around 150. We started at age ten, there being no separate preparatory school, and went on to take School Certificate and, if we stayed the course, the Higher School Certificate.

There was a conventional curriculum. We were taught Latin and French (but no Greek), History, English, Geography, Maths and Chemistry and Physics (but no Biology). The afternoons, except on Wednesdays, were devoted to games, with athletics in the spring and swimming in the big open-air baths in the summer. The games were taken seriously and our fixture list included the main East Anglian independent schools. It was a Church of England school and boys were expected to be confirmed after suitable instruction by the chaplain. There were one or two non-christians and one recalls seeing them, including two Burmese boys, wandering around the museum and the library during the regular morning chapel services.

The Officer Training Corps paraded every Wednesday afternoon. The junior forms were taught carpentry during one period per week and older boys had the option of continuing with carpentry instead of some games. During the morning break every day we did P T under Sergeant-Major Vale's instruction.

My recollection of the nine years I spent at the school is mainly a blurred mass of lessons, exams and games, but a few events come to the front of my mind. One was when the visiting team of German schoolboy hockey players scored a goal. The eleven young Aryans sprang as one to attention when the ball hit the back board, thrust out their right arms and shouted 'Heil Hitler' in exact unison. It was a three-all draw, so we had a triple demonstration of Nazi fervour and had an early, firsthand, intimation of what was to come.

Philip Mead {Hampshire and England} became our cricket coach in the late nineteen-thirties, and though into his forties, he still bowled accurately in the nets and one cannot forget his distinctive batting style, all nudges and pushes but designed to accumulate runs. He demonstrated what a really good coach can do and the eleven became a formidable school side. He was a thoroughgoing old style professional; he qualified to play for Suffolk in their few minor counties matches and seemed invariably to make the century for which he was guaranteed £100.

Discipline at Framlingham was good and essentially self-imposed by prefects and sub-prefects. Their word was law, backed up eventually by house-masters and the headmaster who had a cane but was very rarely called upon to use it. Mr Whitworth, the head, was an austere figure who had an artificial leg - the result of a flying accident in the first world war. He nevertheless was a keen sailor and had a small yacht moored at Pen Mill which he sailed over for Dunkirk to help with the evacuation, only to be turned back when he had got as far as Harwich.

The Reverend Rupert Kneese, second master, had a hockey stick handle which threatened painful punishment, but it was never, to my knowledge, actually used to beat a boy. The standard punishments were to copy out pages of logarithm books or 'walking up and down'. There were boys with good eyesight and a neat writing hand who would copy logarithm pages for a modest fee, say half a Mars bar, for wealthier reprobates. I got my younger sister to read out pages for me and she says that I told her it was for prep. But the walking up and down indignity, which must surely have been unique among public schools, could not be bought off. It involved, literally, walking up and down for stated times in a silent file along the gravel path in front of the school and in full view of the prefects' room window. It was an aimless form of punishment and my house master, Mr Thomas, who had overall charge of playing fields, introduced an alternative - the extraction, from measured plots on the cricket square of plantains and other troublesome weeds. But this could only be a temporary venture into productive punishment.

'Rupe' seemed to have been given, or to have taken on himself, the responsibility for the length of our locks; he would order any boy showing a tendency to long hair to report to Sonny Moore, on his next weekly visit, to have it cut. We were a tidy bunch of boys, in our grey herringbone suits and short back and sides.

It might be thought that education at Framlingham would have instilled a conservative attitude, and in some ways it did. However, in one particular, its influence was quite the opposite. The course for our Higher School certificate was set by the Oxford & Cambridge joint Board and the 'set books' for main subject English included such radical texts as Disraeli's *Two Nations* and Tressel's *The Ragged Trousered Philanthropists* - a book that illuminates the evils of unrestrained capitalism more brightly than Karl Marx.

Framlingham had always been an innovative school. The large open-air swimming pool was installed as early as 1873 and it was one of the first schools to have squash courts. Mr Thomas was a good squash player and taught Norman Borrett the game in these courts - Borrett succeeded Amir Bey, of Egypt, as the open squash champion in later years. Framlingham, was among the first to become co-educational and it was the first public school to appoint, in the 1990s, a female head, Mrs Gwen Randall.

I got a leaving scholarship from Framlingham and a County Major Scholarship from Suffolk and these enabled me to go to the South Eastern Agricultural College at Wye in Kent at the beginning of the war. The county scholarship had strings attached to it - I had to repay part of it as soon as I started earning a salary - but I certainly raised no objection to this and in due course paid back the required instalments out of my Sudan government salary.

My time at Wye was short, just long enough to pass the intermediate exam on the way to a degree. Academically, it broke new ground for me as I had done no biology at Framlingham and I was taken aback when the Reverend Dr Brade-Birks informed us that, this morning, we would be dissecting the frog. The 'phoney war' was coming to an end; we saw dog-fights in the sky and trainloads of exhausted soldiers coming back from Dunkirk. We had to go into cellar shelters when the sirens went, and some bombs landed on the cricket pitch. This was the signal for a move, for the remainder of the course, to Reading University, somewhat further from the front line.

My recollection of the next two years is of a jumble of activities. There were the lectures, of course, with weekly practicals on the University farm at Sonning. I trained in the S T C - the Senior Training Corps - and, for a while, I was in the Home Guard and I'm reminded of our little patrols every time I see Dad's Army on the television. There was a regular fire-watching rota but, although the sirens went quite often, we were never actually bombed and had no incendiaries to deal with. During my last year I took a radio-location [soon to be called radar] course and was interviewed for a post in the navy. However, the powers that be had other ideas and I found myself called up for army service in the Primary Training Wing at the Hyderabad Barracks in Colchester.

The square bashing was nothing new to me but it was something different to find oneself at night sleeping on straw 'biscuits' on the barrack floor. Each of us had three of these thin straw mattresses which we neatly piled, along with folded blanket, at the bed-head at the call of 'rise and shine' each morning. The platoon was recruited from all walks of life and it came as a surprise to me that a few of the recruits could not sign their names. Is the general standard of literacy any better today?

Having mastered the art of dismantling a jammed Bren gun and putting it together again in the dark and having had some practice at firing it and the 303 rifle and throwing Mills bombs on the range, I was whisked away one day on a crowded troop train to the Driver Training Unit at Kinmel Park Camp near Rhyl in North Wales.

We had bunks to sleep in at Kinmel Park, but we continued with square bashing, supported by strenuous gym and I have never been so physically fit as I was after a few weeks there. The technical part of the course was learning to drive the trucks needed to carry radio equipment in the approved army manner and learning how to receive and send Morse code. I have to assume that I was sent to Rhyl as a result of the aptitude tests that we took at the Primary Training Wing. In fact, I found that I could learn Morse reasonably well, but a few others in the platoon seemed to have a real talent for it - a talent that I was to see in full flower within a few short weeks when crossing the North Atlantic in convoy, and watching the Aldis lamps winking.

15

The Post-War Scene

One might have thought that the end of World War II would bring a speedy end to food rationing, but in fact bread rationing was introduced only after the end of the war and the return to normal supplies was much slower than after the first world war.

In 1945 the Minister of Agriculture, R S Hudson, wrote, 'I write to convey my deep thanks and high appreciation to all those who have worked so hard in our food production campaign ..... essential part in achieving victory ..... I can however offer you no prospect of relaxation. Food here and in the world at large is deperately short.' In December of that year, the new Minister of Agriculture, Tom Williams, declared that, 'The world food shortage is extremely serious.' Greater output was required from British farms. The Agricultural Executive Committees, though now shorn of their pre-fix 'War', were to encourage production with the help of a new advisory service.

Farmers were still to be graded for productivity and poor performers were to be 'put under supervision' and if they did not improve, their land would be taken into public ownership and managed by a commission. In

August 1947 the Prime Minister said that the government had decided
on a programme designed to increase the nett agricultural output by one
hundred million pounds, or twenty per cent, by 1951/52.

The Journal of the Ministry of Agriculture for August 1948 reported
that, 'Many farmers will already have seen the figures for the 1949 crop-
ping Programme ..... one of the tasks which the County Agricultural
Executive Committees and their District Committees will be to ensure
..... that every farmer knows the share of the acreage of the various crops
which he is expected to grow on his land.'

The National Agricultural Advisory Service [NAAS, later ADAS]
assumed the duties of the pre-war county services which had varied
widely in size and quality. The form taken by the NAAS owed much to
American influence. Sir James Scott Watson and Sir Robert Rae, who
had been agricultural attaches to the United States during the war, had
been impressed by the American agricultural extension education system, by which the state universities, or land-grant colleges, followed up
their in-college training with 'extension education' among farmers who
had been through the college course. The NAAS found itself with dual
functions - the furtherance of government policy and the provision of
extension education.

The Agricultual Education Association deserves a mention here. It
was set up in the early years of the century mainly for academic staff but
after the last war it attracted membership from the newly formed NAAS
as well as from some commercial organisations. It had a membership of
over 600 at one time and held winter and summer conferences and it had,
since 1924, published a journal - Agricultural Progress - which featured
papers given at the conferences as well as some outside contributions. In
1970 I took on the editorship, little thinking that I would continue in
the job for 27 years. We published once a year and the journal circulated
in many countries. By 1997 the membership of the A E A had dropped
to about 60, partly because it had splintered into a number of specialised
societies and, in spite of changing its name to the Rural Education and
Development Association, it failed to attract members and was wound up.
I declined to banish the unpopular word, agriculture, and the journal kept
its title until the last issue.

Lincolnshire, the county to which I was posted, comprised three 'parts' - Lindsey, Kesteven and Holland - and had always prided itself on agricultural excellence. It was the home of a number of agricultural clubs and societies, with the Lincolnshire Agricultural Society catering for the whole county and organising meetings and the annual Clean Farms Competition. The latter awarded prizes for farms considered best by judges appointed from outside the county, not solely upon freedom from weeds but according to their general appearance of efficiency which might include, for instance, the equipment of the farm workshop. As District Officer for North Kesteven, I was most closely connected with the Metheringham Farmers Discussion Group and its allied Ploughing and Plashing Society, whose chairman was also chairman of the District Agricultural Executive Committee - the redoubtable Alderman George Flintham.

16

Competitions

In addition to acting as secretary to these North Kesteven societies I found myself involved in the Clean Farms Competition. This task was partly due to petrol rationing which was in force for years after the war ended. As a government official, I was given petrol for approved work and this included collecting judges for the competition and ferrying them to all the farms included in the competition, which might be found anywhere between the Humber and the Wash.

There were some notable farms in my 'patch'. Smiths Potato Estates covered some thousands of acres, ranging from the fluffy peat in the fens to Lincolnshire limestone on the 'heath'. Mr Jack Ireson managed both the estate and the farms and it was a huge task. Until the mid fifties horses supplied the motive power and there was a large labour force.

The production of potatoes was the main object and, there being no indoor storage in those days, the crop was lifted and stored in the field in clamps – or 'pies' to use the local term. There were workers on the farm who spent their entire working lives, from one year's end to another, riddling potatoes from these pies to supply suitably graded potatoes to the

Smiths crisping factory in Lincoln. When the freezing winter wind was blowing they would rig a canvas shelter to shield them from the blast. The thousands who munched their way through the tuppeny packets of Smiths Crisps, with their little blue twists of salt, can have had little idea of what went on in the production of the potatoes.

The estate farms were managed in a meticulous manner with complete records being kept in the estate office at Nocton. The clerks sat to their work on high stools, as though in the city, and kept their field-by-field records of all operations and yields in leather-bound ledgers in immaculate copperplate. No-one could have foreseen the coming of the computer.

It so happened that, in the same parish of Nocton, there was a class winner in the 1949 Clean Farms Competition - Mr E M Howard of Nocton Rise. This was a 450-acre farm on the Lincolnshire Limestone 'heath' similar in soil to others on this geological formation but most unusual in that eight generations of the Howard family had occupied it

A PRIZE WINNER IN THE PLOUGHING MATCH . THIS ENTRY ALSO WON THE
PRIZE FOR THE BEST TURNED-OUT PAIR OF HORSES.
PHOTO: LINCS. ECHO.

continuously since 1742. The farm must have been much smaller then because it was not till 1776 that the Lord of the Manor promoted an Act of Parliament for the enclosure of Nocton Heath. White's Directory of Lincolnshire for 1892 records that Dunston Pillar – at the Lincoln end of the heath – was erected as late as 1751, bearing a beacon to guide travellers on its trackless wastes. This beacon was replaced with a statue of George III in 1810 when the rabbit warren of the heath had been enclosed into great, square fields. By 1949, when Mr Howard won the prize, this tall statue had been taken down, being too near an aerodrome built nearby during the last war.

I have recently contacted the farm and learned that Mr E M Howard's grandson is now farming Nocton Rise - the tenth generation to occupy the farm continuously since 1742. However, it is now run in conjun-

A PRIZE WINNING ENTRY IN THE PLASHING COMPETITION. THIS DIFFICULT, OVERGROWN, GAPPY HEDGE WAS A TESTER FOR THE COMPETITORS WHO DREW LOTS FOR THEIR SECTION. THE 'PLASHED' FENCE, KEPT TRIMMED, WOULD BE STOCK-PROOF FOR MANY YEARS AND THE DITCH COULD NOW BE DUG OUT. PHOTO: AUTHOR.

tion with a much larger acreage in order to be economically viable under modern conditions.

The committee met in our office in Guildhall Street, Lincoln, and the paperwork was done there. Finding sites for the competitions was not always easy. Not every farmer wants a considerable part of his land to be ploughed in small - say half acre - competition plots by numerous competitors in several classes; and it was sometimes difficult to find suitable lengths of untidy hedge requiring to be laid ['plashed' was the local term] by perhaps a dozen entries.

In some years the society also ran competitions for the best roots grown in the area or for the best thatched stacks. The photographs give examples of some of the prize-winning work. In some years there was also a prize for the best turned-out pair of horses in the horse ploughing section and

THE FIRST PRIZE WINNER IN THE 1953 THATCHING COMPETITION - MR JOHN SCHOLEY OF WHITE HOUSE FARM, WHISBY, LINCOLN. STACK THATCHING HAS ALMOST DISAPPEARED AS THE COMBINE HARVESTER HAS TAKEN OVER, BUT THE ART OF THATCHING IS STILL THRIVING IN THE ROOFING OF BUILDINGS. PHOTO: AUTHOR.

the District Advisor [as my colleagues and I were known] also had much to do in the organisation of the ploughing and plashing competitions. The above illustration also shows one of the best sets of harness.

In those post-war years, MAFF, through its Advisory Services, supported the agricultural societies, in the belief that their work contributed to agricultural production. Today the local societies and the National Society of Ploughmen receive no government support.

Our well-publicised ploughing matches were popular events and the plashing and thatching competitions were well patronised. These activities of the agricultural societies continue today. The 54th British National Ploughing championship has just been held on a farm near Reading and the director, Mr Ken Chapple, reports that entries and attendance were well up. Some societies, including the Metheringham one, have given up but others have taken their place and there can be no doubt that they contribute to the maintenance of high cultivation standards.

17

Grants & Subsidies

A ROADWAY RENOVATION UNDER FARM IMPROVEMENT SCHEME.

A SET OF FARM BUILDINGS BEFORE AND AFTER REPLACEMENT UNDER THE FARM IMPROVEMENT SCHEME, PHOTOGRAPHED FROM THE SAME POINT

The NAAS, as an arm of government, also had to administer the remarkable series of official schemes that were enacted with a view to increasing production from an industry which still suffered from half a century's neglect. These included the Farm Improvement Scheme under which farmers were paid one third of the cost of capital work such as modernising buildings or renovating·farm roads.

Feeding stuffs for livestock were rationed until 1953 but there was provision, for instance, for an extra allowance of cereals for whey-fed pigs. Licences were needed for the purchase of wire fencing and other materials and all these pieces of legislation had to be administered through the agricultural executive committees. Under the marginal production scheme extra subsidy on fertilisers was obtainable for applications to 'marginal' land, and of course there could be debate as to what was 'marginal', while it was impossible to be absolutely sure that the particular lot of fertiliser was all applied to the said land. There were acreage payments for potato and rye production up till 1950.

There was great emphasis on land drainage at this time, too, with generous grants in aid and specialist drainage officers to help. 'On more than half of the agricultural land in England and Wales field drainage is a fundamental necessity for efficient farming', was the message carried on the series

OLD STYLE DRAINAGE TILES FROM A PREVIOUS AGE OF LAND IMPROVEMENT UNCOVERED DURING GRANT-AIDED DRAINAGE IN LINCOLNSHIRE IN THE 1950's.

of 21 special Drainage Leaflets produced by MAFF.

The Victorians had known this well enough and records show that 12 million acres were drained between 1840 and 1890. Old drainage systems often came to light during the new operations and parts of them could still be made to work. Old drainage tiles were often uncovered; the handmade, interlocking type was not common but the U-shape on flat tile was popular until the latter part of the 19th century. They were superseded by the mechanically extruded round tiles for all the later under drainage.

Improving land drainage became one of the most important tasks of the advisory services and there was a remarkable, year by year, increase in the amount of land receiving grant for under drainage from a mere 15,000 acres in 1940 to 270,000 acres in 1973.

Some of the grants in aid were payable at standard rates or otherwise as a proportion of the farmer's expenditure on the work, supported by documents. Farmers were often allowed to include the cost of their own farm labour and machinery in the grant-aidable expenditure so that the MAFF-funded financial assistance could be considerably more than one third of the out-of- pocket expense on a given scheme.

A FIELD IN LINCOLNSHIRE BEING TILE DRAINED IN A GRANT-AIDED
MAFF SCHEME.

Hedge removal was also grant-aided at this time when agricultural efficiency was the talisman. There were really far too many hedges in some districts for the economical use of machinery, not to mention the amount of potentially productive land that hedges occupied. It is a sign of the times that DEFRA is now [2003] giving farmers grants for the planting of hedgerows, improved 'habitat' for wild life is now more important than agricultural output.

HEDGE REMOVAL IN LINCOLNSHIRE
SUBSIDISED BY MAFF

18

The Small Farmer Scheme

The Small Farmer Scheme was introduced in the late 1950s by John Hare, Minister of Agriculture in the Conservative government. In a speech to the Farmers Club he said, 'the whole country would be immeasurably poorer if the small farmer went under.' This sentiment, with its background of regard for the 'English yeoman' lies behind much legislation. It finds expression, for instance, in the Small Holdings and Allotment Act of 1920. County Councils were encouraged, and given grants in aid, to buy up large farms and divide them into small holdings which were to be tenanted by men who had been thrown out of work in the post-war depression. A Smallholders' Association was formed with government and private backing, to set up similar schemes. Economic viability was to be ensured by compulsory arrangements for co-operative buying and selling. These well-meaning endeavours ran into difficulties. Although they concentrated on intensive enterprises such as pigs, poultry and horticulture, the tenants found it difficult or impossible to make a decent living. Disillusioned smallholders from industrial areas found it hard to fit in to rural society and the locals were envious of the special favours accorded to the interlopers, many of whom preferred to return home and live on the dole.

Allotments, which have a long history, have been more successful, and an interesting recent survey among the tenants of some 32 allotments run by Oxford City Council has shown up some of the motives of the holders. Demand for allotments is high and the following is an extract from a recently published report.

'Most surprising is the number of high flyers who rent an allotment. We prefer organic, they claim, and discover, as a bonus, that the allotment gives them time for reflection, allowing a return to an earlier, less frantic rhythm of life, away from the high tech, and breakneck speed of their working week. They leave behind their computers and mobile 'phones, dig a little, think a little, and enjoy a cup of tea within the undemanding shelter of the allotment shed. Finally, refreshed and renewed, they take a last proud look at their handiwork, before gathering up a succulent, home grown offering to show off for supper.' This panegyric may not amount to a call for a widespread return to yeoman farming, but it does set out some

A TYPICAL SMALL FARMSTEAD IN SOUTH-WEST SHROPSHIRE. 1959.
PHOTO: AUTHOR.

of the attractions of going 'back to the land'.

Under John Hare's scheme, the 'small farms' had to produce 3-5 year plans, with budgets designed to improve profitability. Eligibility depended partly on acreage and partly on the test of Standard Man Days - SMDs were based on the average labour required for the various crops and types of livestock. 'Naturally', the Journal of the Ministry said, 'there will be difficulties and some anomalies. Each farm is different and will be considered separately by the NAAS officers'. The definition certainly left room for discussion in many cases, but there were estimated to be 90,000 eligible farms in the country.

There were more of these small farms in the west than in Lincolnshire and I had to deal with many cases when I was transferred to Shropshire in 1959. I described the way of life of these farmers, based on a survey of 28 of them in the south-west of the county, in an article in the NAAS Quarterly Review, from which the following extracts are taken.

'All but one of the farmhouses are built of local stone and are of considerable age, a few still having antique fireplaces open to the sky. All but four have earth closets and only one has a bathroom. It is clear that most need extensive and costly improvements if they are to reach accepted modern standards. They produce a substantial proportion of their food on the farm. They normally have milk from one of their cows for most of the year, keep some laying hens and grow their own potatoes and swedes. Ten of them still kill a pig and cure their own bacon, but this practice seems to be dying out.

Is it a healthy life? Asked if they had been off work during the past twelve months, 23 replied, 'No'. Ten farmers mentioned previous ailments, in three cases resulting from strains or fractures. Almost all agreed that theirs was a healthy life. Asked when they last had a holiday away from home, most of these farmers and their wives responded with a wry smile. Only one of the 28 takes one week's holiday per annum. Most have not spent a night off the farm since they started farming or went on their honeymoon.'

I went on to describe, in this article, the education of the children - 58 born to 22 of the families, of whom 28 were still at school, 23 having left and 7 under school age. Of those still at school, 11 were at primary, 11 at secondary and 6 at grammar school. For their secondary education most of the children had to travel up to a dozen miles or more by school bus and it was very common for children to leave modern or grammar schools at the minimum leaving age; the boys in particular seemed to be brought home to help with the work.

The small farm question was taken seriously by the whole industry at that time. The Farmers Weekly magazine bought a small farm, Broadley, at Llantony, near Abergavenny to research the economics of the business and, if possible, demonstrate profitable changes in the system. We took some of our clients there in July, 1961. but it has to be admitted that the F W, like the rest of us, found that there was no magic wand to bring greater prosperity to the small farmer. The grants payable under the Scheme in south west Shropshire, where I dealt with over 80 schemes between 1959 and 1961, averaged £780 per farm over the 5-year period [very low, even allowing for inflation] and it was not possible to introduce major changes.

The Small Farmer Scheme had admirable objectives, but the hard fact is that it could not halt the inexorable trend towards larger farming units.

The change to metrication has meant that DEFRA has altered the size categories of surveyed farms so that precise comparisons are not possible. However, we can compare the number of farms on the 20-100 acre bracket [approximately 8-40 hectares] in 1950, which was 103,474, with the number in the 5-40 hectare category in 2003, which was 60,022. These MAFF/DEFRA statistics show that we have probably lost about half of our small farms in the past fifty years. Moreover, many of the remaining small farms are dependent on various forms of diversification for their survival.

The Farmers Weekly has itself been caught up in the seemingly unstoppable move towards larger farming units. Their Easton Lodge farm has been amalgamated with another East Anglian farm, Sacrewell Lodge, and the farm accountants describe approvingly, in the F W issue of the week 9th - 15th January, 04, how they have thus been able to reduce their overheads per hectare - an essential step in their search for economic viability.

A SMALL FARM KITCHEN IN SHROPSHIRE - IMPROVED UNDER SMALL FARMER SCHEME.

19

Grassland Improvement

After World War 2, MAFF called for a special campaign to improve production from grassland and we even called in experts from New Zealand where they were good at producing milk economically from grass.

It is difficult at the time of writing, when there is a 'milk lake' in Europe as a result of overproduction, and farm prices for milk are low, to recall the post-war decades when the country, through MAFF, was exhorting the farming industry to improve the productivity of our grassland - which was certainly in a poor state, full of creeping bent and Yorkshire fog, lacking in clover and under fertilised. The Welsh Plant Breeding Station, whose director, Sir George Stapledon, received a knighthood for his work, was breeding new types of herbage. White and red clovers, ryegrasses, timothy s, cocksfoots and fescues were bred and seeds mixtures to suit all requirements were advocated. The seeds had to be multiplied and herbage seed production became important.

The advisory services were in the thick of these activities and every year we went on an indoctrination course to Aberystwyth where we learned how to identify types of clovers and grasses and to spot the weeds

WEIGHING PRODUCTION FROM GRASS TRIAL PLOTS IN THE MIDLANDS, 1961

which could contaminate herbage seed.

The conservation of grass for winter feeding has always been a chancy business, the weather in June - the main hay making month - being unreliable. For many years silage had been advocated as an alternative method of grass conservation, but handling the heavy green material was laborious and too many silages were butyric from excess moisture or overheated and brown from being too dry and over-aerated. In 1965 a new system - brought to this country by a Mr Delahunty, also from New Zealand - came on the scene.

The green forage was enclosed in a large plastic container from which the air was pumped out, thus stopping further, wasteful fermentation. The product was known as 'vacuum silage'. and the NAAS demonstrated the system at several centres. A firm specialising in uses for plastic, in Wiltshire, began producing kits for making this vacuum silage and, as they were able to give us the addresses of all purchasers, we could test the effectiveness

A WELL-ATTENDED DEMONSTRATION OF VACUUM SILAGE IN DEVON, 1965. PHOTO: AUTHOR

of demonstrations in a unique manner. Vacuum silage had been given country-wide publicity in the farming press but the marked concentration of vacuum silage-making farms around the sites of the well attended demonstrations showed how effective such demonstrations could be in triggering action.

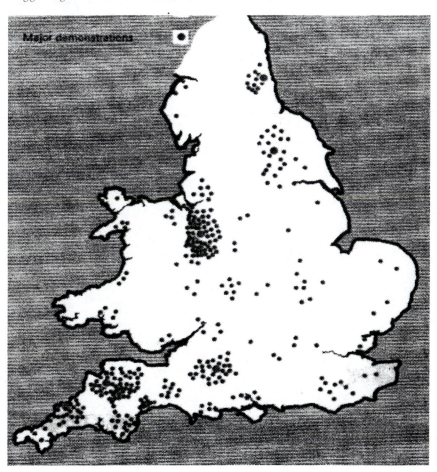

As it happened, the making of true vacuum silage never took on. It was almost impossible to maintain the vacuum for long because of damage by birds or rodents. However, the mere wrapping of silage in plastic prevented both air and moisture from getting in and the use of plastic envelopes for silage became almost universal and has made possible an enormous improvement in silage quality. Silage clamps, enclosed in plastic sheets, have largely taken over from hay making, and these clamps are now commonly 'grazed' by cattle along their feeding face. It has been a true revolution in the practice of grass conservation and ruminant nutrition.

20

Extensive Education

On the educational side, MAFF's Advisory Service provided a free soil sampling and analysis service. Sometimes this was offered to help to explain crop failures but often in order to let farmers know whether their land met normal nutritional standards for lime, phosphate and potash. I did over 200 samples per annum and it could be interesting and useful work, but I could not understand why, in contrast for instance with the Dutch, we did not make at least a nominal charge.

After a few years one became something of an expert, with the help of our divisional chemists, entomologists and plant pathologists, in diagnosing crop ailments and, where possible, in prescribing control measures. There were many causes of crop damage, which varied from the more common such as potato root eelworm or wheat bulb fly to the less usual such as gout fly or manganese deficiency. This 'crop doctoring' service was one of the most interesting aspects of advisory work in those days and was much appreciated by farmers.

In this crop doctoring part of the work, did I ever give wrong advice? It would be presumptuous indeed to claim never and as one example I recall a crop of winter wheat in Wellingore parish, badly thinned by the little white maggots of the wheat bulb fly. [This was before the advent of insecticides to control this pest.] I recommended the farmer to plough the crop up and resow with spring barley. He did this but there followed a wet spring making it difficult to work down a good seed bed for the barley which turned out to be a very poor crop. With the benefit of experience, I became more cautious in giving this sort of advice and I would have done better, in that Wellingore case, to advise a good dressing of nitrogen to encourage the wheat to grow away from the pest damage.

THE ADVISORY SERVICE TOOK MANY THOUSANDS OF SOIL SAMPLES. PHOTO: AUTHOR.

Winter wheat has a great capacity for tillering - one plant can produce ten or twenty or even more ear-bearing shoots under fertile conditions. There was a saying in Lincolnshire that, 'if an old sheep can't lie down without touching a wheat plant, the growing crop is thick enough to leave'.

We did many field trials to test crop varieties, fertilisers, pesticides and herbicides. These would be sited where possible alongside less busy roads so that farmers could inspect them. I remember particularly the herbicide trial in my first season with MAFF. It was to test the new growth regulator, or 'hormone' weed killer - MCPA. It signalled another revolution in farming. Those of us who had been brought up to hand- or horse-hoe weeds were amazed to see the way the 'hormone' weed killer demolished broad-leaved weeds in a cereal crop. A host of new, selective herbicides soon came on to the market and we demonstrated most of them in local trials.

During my years in North Kesteven we ran an exhibit every Friday in Lincoln Corn Exchange. The old exchange hall was used as a cinema on most days but the seats were wheeled out on Fridays and 150 trade stalls brought in. MAFF hired one of these and we put on an exhibit dealing with some topical technical matter or government regulation; we were always busy talking to merchant or farmers, of whom there would be about 500

THERE WERE 59 EAR-BEARING TILLERS ON THIS ONE PLANT OF CAPELLE WHEAT.

A SPRING BARLEY VARIETY TRIAL BEING HARVESTED. THE 'PUSHER' TYPE OF COMBINE HARVESTER, SHOWN HERE, GREATLY SIMPLIFIED THE TAKING OF YIELDS. PHOTO: AUTHOR

We always had suitable leaflets on the table and up to 50 would be taken up if the subject was of wide interest. On this subject of leaflets, one should mention the very fine series of around 1000 advisory leaflets published by the ministry over a quarter of a century dealing with a huge variety subjects, including, for instance, a number about birds of agricultural significance. These leaflets were regularly revised and were a mine of information, but their publication has ceased. Just one is shown below to give an idea of appearance and layout.

We worked closely with the local press in those days and I had a good relationship with the farming editor of the Lincolnshire Echo. He would include articles on farm visits, demonstrations or other developments, often with photographs, in his weekly page. I am indebted to him for some of the photographs in this chapter. Another sign of the times is that these farming pages have disappeared from local newspapers. It was a time for demonstrating and publicising the many advances in practice that the research stations and experimental husbandry farms were working out.

We advisors took our work very seriously in those days when improved agricultural output was called for. We did much work out of normal hours,

LINCOLN CORN EXCHANGE ON MARKET DAY, 1955.
PHOTO: LINCS. ECHO.

43

Advisory Leaflet **43**
Amended 1977

MINISTRY OF AGRICULTURE, FISHERIES AND FOOD

Natural Hatching

FOR the small poultry keeper who wants to raise a few chicks but does not want the bother and expense of even a small incubator, natural hatching under a broody hen is the ideal way. It is, however, essentially dependent on having a broody or broodies when required.

Hatching eggs are best obtained from a source of known repute, and in particular the breeding stock should have been blood tested for such egg transmitted diseases as *Pullorum* disease. The eggs for normal hatching are normally sold by the sitting (twelve to fifteen eggs), and the buyer is advised to inquire about the procedure for replacement of infertile eggs when considering purchase.

It is unwise to assume that an apparently broody hen will sit, so it is best to give her a few dummy eggs for a start, and only substitute the genuine sitting after two or three days if she shows a real intention to brood. It is always advisable to give her the eggs—dummy or genuine—in the evening, rather than during the day, as this is less likely to put her off sitting.

Preparation of the Nest

If the hen has picked her own nest and it is in a convenient and safe place, she should be left on it. Otherwise, a nest or box should be prepared where it is convenient, and

AN ADVISORY EXHIBIT IN LINCOLN CORN EXCHANGE. ON THE LEFT,
MR PHILLIPSON, FIELD OFFICER OF THE BARDNEY SUGAR FACTORY. PHOTO:
LINCS. ECHO.

often during evenings and weekends, with discussion groups and Young
Farmers' Clubs.

At the time of writing, when agricultural production hardly seems to
matter and the very word 'agriculture' has been left out of the title of
MAFF's successor, the Department for Environment, Food and Rural
Affairs [DEFRA]; when the Journal of the Ministry of Agriculture,
produced monthly since 1893, has folded, it is with something like in-
credulity that I look back on those post-war years of great activity when I
worked for MAFF in North Kesteven.

One thing, however, is now clear. The policy of successive govern-
ments and of MAFF during those post-war years - a policy of growing
more at home to save foreign exchange, while keeping down the price of
food, was successful. The infrastructure of agriculture which had been so
long neglected was vastly changed with the help of grants, and the adop-
tion of new techniques revolutionised the productivity of the industry

so that it became a European leader in this respect. Another result is that fewer than 2 per cent of the country's working population are now directly engaged in agriculture so that the industry has less clout in the voting power of our democracy.

Food shortages have passed and we have arrived at a time when obesity has taken their place as a cause for public concern and it is reported that one third of our food is going to waste.

DEMONSTRATION PLOTS AND NAAS TENT AT THE
LINCOLNSHIRE COUNTY SHOW.

21

The Lighter Side of Working for MAFF

One bitterly cold day in March 1950 I was working on the quarterly agricultural returns when Harry Wilkinson, who farmed at the bottom of Oakshott Fen, clumped up the bare wooden stairs. I knew him because he had recently been given a permit to buy strychnine, needed to put on the bodies of worms to be laid as poison bait in mole runs. It was not about this that Harry had come, but about the Caythorpes' chickens from across the rhine. I should explain that there are no hedges in the bleak, black fen and the land is divided by long straight drainage channels known as rhines, pronounced reens.

Harry and I exchanged civilities and he remarked that the going would be hard for the Lincolnshire Handicap in this, the last season when this handicap would open the flat racing season at Lincoln. But he soon came to the point of his visit. 'I'm fed up with the Caythorpes' chickens,' he said. 'They are for ever flying over the rhine and scratting around my corn stacks and now they're eating half the ration of mash that I put down for my breeding hens'. He wanted me to get the Committee to order the

Caythorpes to control their thieving poultry.

I listened sympathetically. It would take weeks for a permit for chicken wire to come through. I wondered aloud if he could catch the marauding fowl and clip their wings to stop them flying over the rhine. And I tried to side-step the problem by suggesting that he might consult Mr Melton, the local NFU secretary.

It was not a complete surprise when, a few weeks later, a disturbed Jim Caythorpe stumped up my stairs, He and his wife, he told me, had been doing their level best to build up a small laying flock and thus increase the nation's egg production, and had until recently been getting good results. Then, suddenly, only yesterday, some of his birds had started dying. He wanted me to go out and see the birds and perhaps arrange for post mortems. I found myself again prevaricating. Hens could die from many causes, I said. Had they been getting proper rations? Were his birds on free range and did they stray? "I don't know if they stray,' he said. 'I'll have to ask the missus',

He had barely left the office when who should arrive but Harry Wilkinson, looking really agitated. Without preliminaries he told me that he had finally come to the conclusion that he could no longer afford to feed his neighbour's hens. He had shut up his own birds, mixed strychnine with some mash and laid it along his side of the rhine. Some of his neighbour's hens had flown over and eaten the mash with fatal results. Alarmed and dismayed at the result of his action, he and his dog had scared the invaders back to their rightful side and he had cleared up the poisoned mash. I said I would come down and see him as soon as I could. In fact I went to the Fen the next day and, as I drove along the canal side, past the scene of the dispute I could see a long line of brand new 4-foot chicken wire erected along the rhine bank on the Caythorpes' side and glinting in the sun. How, I wondered, had he got that wire. The Committee had certainly not given him a permit to buy it.

I had another diverting encounter a few years later, this time in connection with the Small Farmer Scheme. I had been to the farm several times and had got to know the occupier well. He was a go-ahead man in his early thirties and lived in a solid stone house with his mother. On this visit he invited me into the kitchen and, over a cup of tea, informed me that he intended to get married. His mother wasn't getting any younger and he thought it would be as well to have a younger woman about the place. This business was, strictly speaking, outside my remit but I was happy to murmur my approval.

'As a matter of fact', he said, 'I put an advert in the Farmers Weekly six weeks ago.' He pulled a press cutting from his wallet and it read, 'Progressive young farmer seeks acquaintance with young woman, view to marriage. 95 acres, modernised farm house, developing under Small Farmer Scheme. Future wife should understand farming and contribute to capital requirements. Please supply photographs'.

He refilled my cup and again referred to his wallet, bringing out nine photographs and laying them on the kitchen table. 'I got my first reply within four days', he said, 'and the last about a fortnight ago. They took a bit of weighing up', he said and invited my comments on the gallery. I bent my professional skills to this task, but it was immediately obvious that number 6 must be the winner. They all looked attractive, but this one was stunningly good-looking. 'Yes', said the young farmer, when he saw that I had at once picked out number 6. 'I thought she was the one and I was writing to ask her down when I thought I'd better ask my mother.' It seemed that she had only glanced at the photographs, but had spent an afternoon carefully going through the letters. She vetoed number 6 out of hand. Number 3, she said, was the one for him. 'You see', he said, 'Myrtle has twelve good Aberdeen Angus suckler cows and twenty followers'. There was nothing I could say to that, and he was, in any case, already calling her by her Christian name.

The next time I went to the farm, I heard that Myrtle had been down and that the two young people had got on well. His mother had taken twenty acres of grass keep in the next parish on her own initiative and Myrtle had sent down her cattle. With their addition to the stock already on the farm there was no doubt that the requirement for stocking under the Small Farmer Scheme would be met and the banns were to be read for the first time the following Sunday. The Farmers Weekly had done a useful service and their Farmlife section continues to bring couples together through its personal columns - a photograph in the issue of 24 Feb. 2003 shows Iain and Jane -'a match made through F W.'

It was not unknown for farmers to employ some subterfuge to obtain some of the grants. I remember an application for a supplementary drainage grant on a Lincolnshire farm. There was a basic grant of £1 per chain but, if the land could be classified as 'marginal', the grant was doubled. A Ministry official known as a Land Commissioner [L. C.] had to inspect the land to decide if it was marginal. The applicant in this case was a distinctly well-off young man who hunted four days a week in the winter and normally drove a high-powered car.

He and I and the L. C. were to rendezvous, not at his fine house on the escarpment, but in the low fields by the Witham where the applicant farmed a large area of grass land with several miles of ditches that needed clearing. I arrived first, followed by the L C, and then a battered Morris Minor came down the lane. I was a little surprised when out stepped the hunting man now arrayed in dirty fustian trousers and a ragged raincoat. He had the grace to slip me a rather guilty grin as I introduced him to the L C and we inspected the land along a route which showed up patches of tussock grass and reeds. The applicant really had no need to appear to be less than well-off and in due course the land was certified as marginal and the supplementary grant paid.

One thought may cross the reader's mind. When so many grants and subsidies had to pass through the official's hand, was there ever any sign of bribery and corruption? I can only say that the possibility did not show its head in all my years in the service of MAFF except, perhaps, for one incident. One afternoon at our stand in the Corn Exchange I was handed an envelope by a farmer which I only opened at the end of the day's business. The envelope contained, if I remember correctly, a £5 note and a few lines to say that the farmer much appreciated the help that I had given him. I chased off to his farm that evening and left a message of thanks under the windscreen wiper of his car, [he being out on the farm] saying that I could not accept his well-meant gift. This may have embarrassed him and he never mentioned it later.

22

Straw Burning & Straw Use

Burning wheat straw after combine-harvesting.
Photo: Farmers Weekly.

An understandable cause for farmers' unpopularity after World War II was the way in which they turned to burning straw in the field. It was a problem that arose out of the move from harvesting with the binder, where the whole crop was brought from the field to the farmstead for threshing, to the combine harvester when only the grain was brought to the store and the straw was left lying in the field. The field burning controversy raged for some forty years and I have many protesting cuttings taken from local and national papers during that period.

Some early models of combine harvesters [such as the German Claas] were fitted with a mechanism which tied the threshed straw into bundles as it emerged from the thresher and dumped them for later collection. But, in the post-war world of specialisation, livestock were no longer kept on many arable farms to tread down straw to make manure, the ingredients of which were much more easily applied in the form of 'artificial' fertilisers. So the Claas type of straw bundler never took on.

However, straw had to be removed to clear the land for following cultivations and farmers found a quick and easy way was to apply a match. With a favourable breeze, there would be nothing left on the field but the ash from the stubble and straw. Neighbours complained vociferously when the smoke and ash blew across their clothes lines; there were also complaints when the smoke blew across roads. It was not unknown for sparks to blow into and ignite nearby standing corn and at least one farmer had his house burned down as a result of sparks blown from a field burn. A cauliflower grower in Lincolnshire reported that a fieldful of his product had been rendered unsalable by smuts landing on the crop.

There were hundreds of less good-humoured letters of complaint in

A SURPRISINGLY GOOD-HUMOURED CARTOON . JIM NEEDLE, OXFORD MAIL, SEPTEMBER, 1984.

both national and local press at this time and the following is just one such exasperated note from an Oxfordshire paper.

'Last floating charred straw'

Sir,

I have resisted the impulse to write to you for several weeks
but today was the last floating charred straw.
Smoke from the burning stubble permeates the atmosphere
- our houses, clothes and lungs, and black straw ash is everywhere.
It is just as bad as last year and the farmers have a bumper
crop to stockpile in the Common Market while thousands
starve all over the world and we suffer pollution.
The fields are black, wild creatures and their habitat destroyed.
It must stop now.

J A Hammond
Steventon Road,
Drayton

Straw burning in the field became extremely unpopular with the public, but the National Farmers Union [NFU] backed its arable farming membership and defended the practice.

MAFF itself was inclined to side with the burners in the belief that field burning kept down the cost of cereal growing.

Our straw burning problems even claimed space in the American press. The Christian Science Monitor had a long article syndicated in the U.S.A. entitled, 'Field burning ignites debate among British'.

Having been brought up on a Suffolk wheat and bean farm where all our crops were cut by binder and the straw was saved, it always seemed to me that straw burning in the field was wrong. There is something attractive about a stack of clean wheat straw - it is springy and most pleasant to lie on. We used a fair proportion of the best of it for stack thatching and the rest, with the barley straw and bean haulms, went for stock bedding and the production of manure.

It was on my UNICEF visit to Greece that I saw the paper mill at Larissa. Wheat straw from the little farms in the plain of Thessaly went in at one end and fine paper came out at the other. It was seeing this that turned me into a straw use specialist in MAFF and I had some encouragement from the ministry.

MAFF and the NFU, while continuing to support the arable farmer's right to field-burn an annual estimated total of 7 million tonnes of surplus straw, were still interested in searching for an economic alternative and allowed me to seek better methods in Europe and to organise several international conferences on straw use. I found interesting examples of apparently economic uses, in addition to the Greek initiative mentioned above In Spain and Italy there were several mills making paper from straw; at Hollabrunn in Austria a farmers' co-operative was making most of that country's French-frieds from a factory to which they supplied not only the potatoes but also the straw fuel with which to cook them; in Denmark whole districts were supplied with hot water from co-operatively run straw-fuelled boiler houses; in County Kerry in Ireland farmers were using some of their limited supplies of straw to soak up effluent from silage.

In England our biggest industrial user of straw at this time was the Stramit factory near Stowmarket which made a type of thick, insulating board from compressed wheat straw. Apart from this, there were traditional uses, for instance for thatching, and other crafts such as straw plait, archery targets and chair backs.* The army no longer seemed to need straw for the 'biscuit' mattresses that I once slept on at the Hyderabad barracks in Colchester.

Straw as fuel seemed a possible bulk use option, particularly when there was a demand for energy from renewable sources. But there is the inherent problem with straw [as for all carbohydrate materials] that it has only half the calorific value of coal and a third that of fuel oil. It becomes

* See also Straw and Straw Craftsmen: Arthur Staniforth, Shire Publications, 2nd Ed. 1991

competitive when the price of Brent crude approaches $30 a barrel and when the straw can be transported and stored at a low moisture content reasonably cheaply. Some dozens of U K farmers installed straw burners, having been set a good example at Ditchingham Hall, Suffolk, by Earl Ferrers when he was Minister of State at MAFF. But only a few have kept going over a period when oil prices have greatly fluctuated and have often been below $20 a barrel.

For all our effort in staging conferences, publishing reports and personal contacts, we have not succeeded in promoting a large commercial take-up of our surplus straw. It has been disappointing, in particular, that the paper industry continues to rely on timber and some recycled paper, for its raw material. Could the government have given more encouragement, with grants and subsidies, as it has done for the use of poultry litter for electricity generation?

The government was indeed finally forced by the weight of public opinion to ban the field burning sf straw, under the Environmental Protection Act of 1990. This has led, not to increased baling and removal for commercial use, but to the almost universal use of straw choppers, fitted to combines, which cut up the straw as it leaves the combine's drum and scatters it over the field so that it can be cultivated without clogging the machinery. There were prophets of doom who said that ploughed-in straw would not break down properly in some soils, but incorporation appears to have been widely successful. So ended one of the most serious controversies that the advisory services had to deal with in post-war agriculture and the furore has now been largely forgotten.

FARMERS — FROM FOOD PRODUCERS TO PARK-KEEPERS

23

European Visits

During service with MAFF I was lucky enough to be released, on 'approved employment terms', to work for the Organisation for European Economic Co-operation [OEEC] for a year [1954/55] based in Paris and , later, for a few months with UNESCO in Greece.

The OEEC was the forerunner of later moves towards European integration. Improved productivity and more co-operation were the order of the day in those post-war years and the Americans, through their Marshall Plan, were very much behind it. I travelled daily from our flat on the rue d'Assas, overlooking the Jardin du Luxembourg, across Paris to the prestigious OEEC headquarters in the Chateau de la Muette, close by the Bois de Boulogne. I worked in the Division for Productivity in Agriculture on Project 48 which was designed to spread the best methods of agricultural education and advice [or,'Extension' as the Americans called it.]. This involved three of us visiting European countries to see what their methods were, organising a conference to exchange all the information and producing a handbook on 'extension' methods in several languages at the end of the project.

Dr Rheinwald was a professor at the University of Hohenheim - he had been in the German army when it tried to grow food in occupied Ukraine, with partisans to contend with, and he did not like to talk about it. A more charming man and one less likely to be a nazi sympathiser it would be difficult to imagine. Monsieur Bonnal, the French member of our trio, had been a prisoner of war but seemed to bear no grudges and we made a congenial group as we travelled from country to country.

Two Americans from land-grant colleges - the homes of United States agricultural 'extension' - were seconded to our division. Mr Richwine, from a midwest college, had a procedure which I have never seen elsewhere. He carried a pack of axiom-loaded cards in his hip pocket which he produced when faced with a knotty problem and he riffled through them till he came upon a solution. I do not recall the exact nature of the problem encountered on one occasion, but I remember that he leafed through the pack until he came to the solution card which said, 'Give credit where credit is due.'

Monsieur Mahou was a French 'vulgarisateur' - extension worker- who took part in Project 48. He was from Lorraine and was an expert in the production of wine and cognac but had no interest at all in liqueurs or martinis which he dismissed as 'women's drinks'. He had another attitude to the fair sex which seemed to prevail among French people at this time. His daughter had a steady boy friend but, apparently, little prospect of ever marrying him. Her marriage had already been arranged with another man who would better suit the family's circumstances. My French friends tell me that this tradition of arranged marriages is now quite out of date in France.

Our division produced a quarterly review entitled FATIS, short for Food and Agriculture Technical Information Service, in English, French and German which carried articles sent in by country liaison officers. An Irishman, Frank McDermott, worked on this review and, in the best tradition of international friendship, he kept a packet of Sinn Fein literature in his drawer. He would bring out his map of Ireland, with a small orange excrescence in the north-east corner, and expatiate on the hardships inflicted on his country by the 'economic war' and other Anglo-Irish disputes. He must have thought that I, having an Irish mother, would be fertile ground

Another Frenchman that I remember well was the gendarme at the end of the Pont de l'Alma. It was soon after the French government had banned the general use of motor horns, because of the awful cacophony that had been filling the streets. On my way home from the Chateau, the horn button on my little Ford Prefect became jammed and I could not stop it hooting as I crossed the bridge, to the great amusement of the traffic man. Would one of our police have shown such a sense of humour?

Our three-man group found something of interest in every country we visited. The Norwegians, for instance, had been treating straw with alkali for many years to improve its digestibility, there being a chronic shortage of pasture for grass conservation in that country. The Dutch had an ingenious method of covering silage, as shown in the illustration. Curiously, at the time of writing, some fifty years after our three man tour, there is an item in the Farmers Weekly of Oct. 15 - 21, 2004, under the heading, 'New Products, Silage pits go under water', which describes a method of 'covering silage pits with a water-filled blanket'.

But old-fashioned methods prevailed in many areas. In Austria the women in hilly areas were still making hay in small cocks on drying

DUTCH METHOD OF SEALING SILAGE.

HAY MAKING IN A MOUNTAINOUS AREA: AUSTRIA, 1954.

BESIDE THE AUTOBAHN IN SOUTHERN GERMANY, 1954, THE INCONGRUOUS
SIGHT OF OX-DRAWN AND HAND CULTIVATION IN A DISTRICT OF FRAGMENTED
FARMS.

frames. In southern Germany we encountered the problem of tiny strip holdings. The problem of fragmented and scattered holdings - the result of local inheritance laws - was widespread in several European countries, whereas in the U K there remained very few examples. In fact, the open field system of scattered strips was such an unusual relic of the past that MAFF, in 1952, took over the parish of Laxton in Nottinghamshire in order to preserve it as a museum of the old strip farming system. On the continent at this time fragmentation was presenting a widespread and serious obstacle to farming progress and a huge legislative effort was needed to effect the consolidation of holdings into manageable blocks- 'remembrement' as the French called it.

In Holland we saw another side of their farming industry, the horse-drawn wagons of churns at the milk factory, brought in from the farms .

A few years later, at a time when we were burning good straw in the field in England, I came across a factory in Austria which supplied almost all the French-fried potatoes in that country. It was run by a co-operative

DUTCH MILK FACTORY, 1954.

CONSERVATION – THE HARD WAY. A DUTCH FARMER DREDGES HIS DYKES
AND TAKES THE BOATLOAD OF SLUDGE TO BE SPREAD BACK ON HIS LAND.
PHOTO: AUTHOR.

MINISTRY OF AGRICULTURE, FISHERIES AND FOOD

FARMING ABROAD

"IMPRESSIONS OF FARMING IN THE U.S.A."
by C. L. BEMBRIDGE, ESQ.

"IMPRESSIONS OF EUROPEAN FARMING"
by A. R. STANIFORTH, ESQ.
(illustrated by lantern slides)

VILLAGE HALL, DUNSTON
WEDNESDAY, 8th FEBRUARY, 1956, at 7.30 p.m.

Chairman : ALDERMAN G. FLINTHAM, M.B.E.

All interested are cordially invited to attend

NATIONAL AGRICULTURAL ADVISORY SERVICE
4095   IN CONJUNCTION WITH METHERINGHAM DISCUSSION GROUP

THE NAAS DID ITS BEST TO PUBLICISE THE INFORMATION GLEANED FROM
OVERSEAS, IN THE PRESS AND AT MEETINGS SUCH AS THAT SHOWN ABOVE.

of farmers who supplied not only the potatoes but also the straw which was used as fuel. In Denmark whole districts were supplied with hot water from co-operative straw-fuelled boiler houses and the French copied the Danish system in a district heating scheme for the Ville Parisi suburb of Paris. We never attempted anything as large as this with straw in the U K but , as mentioned in an·earlier chapter, a number of smaller schemes were installed. In spite of much persuasion, the British paper industry has continued to rely on wood pulp and recycled paper for its raw material.

I had another assignment in Europe at the end of 1973. My 'approved employment' was to assist with plans for the new Schools of Agricultural Technology, known by their Greek initials as KATE. The proposed sites were to be in Athens, Thessaloniki, Larissa and Heraclion in Crete, so I had a great opportunity to see much of Greece.

I had a little excitement, too, while working in that country. When I got there, Greece was ruled by a military junta with the notorious Colonel Papadopulos as its head, but there were important elements determined to overthrow the dictatorship. At the start of my assignment I went up to Thessaloniki and found a room in a city hotel. I as yet spoke no Greek and the hotel people spoke little or no English. On my first morning – a non-working Saturday – I determined to see something of the city, including the turkish quarter in the north. As I left the hotel, I noticed a great deal of pedestrian movement in the street and all the buses were crowded - I assumed that there was some special occasion. I walked through the city and saw the picturesque old Turkish houses. On my return, I could not help noticing that the streets were absolutely empty, except for small knots of soldiers at some street corners. I walked steadily on and occa-sionally saw curious eyes looking at me from behind curtained windows. These people, I thought, must indulge in a long, universal siesta. It was not until I got back to the hotel that I learned that I, a mad Englishman, had blithely traversed a city which the military junta had just put under strict curfew. I bought a short wave radio the next morning so that the BBC overseas service could keep me informed of events.

It was not long after my escapade that the colonels' regime was overthrown in a bloodless revolution. It happened quite suddenly. One morning I came down from my room to find that every photograph of

Colonel Papadopulos - hitherto prominently displayed in every shop or office - had disappeared.

My approved employment in Greece provided more proof that travel broadens the mind. It was a surprise to find that cotton, as well as bananas, were grown in that country. The summer climate was so hot that I could understand how the many Greek tradesmen with whom I had done business in the Sudan managed to withstand the heat of that country for many years, without home leave, Another eye-opener was the proliferation of tiny individual holdings in the plain of Thessaly, holdings that had been provided for the refugees from Greek enclaves in Turkey at the time of the Smyrna massacres in the early nineteen twenties.

A Greek initiative that impressed me was the mill at Larissa which made paper from wheat straw, much of which came from those little farms in Thessaly. At a time when we in England were burning on the field many millions of tons of combine-harvested straw, here in Greece they were feeding wheat straw in at one end of the mill and turning out rolls of excellent paper at the other end.

During my stay at Larissa, one of my Greek hosts invited me to join a Sunday service at the Greek Orthodox cathedral. I could not understand the prayers and sermon, but it was a striking occasion, with a packed congregation. The chanting was magnificent and the varied bright colours of the priestly vestments were startlingly brilliant. However, it was a surprise to find that males and females were strictly segregated, with all the men on the right and the women on the left.

24

Organic Farming

This book is about what actually happened on farms in the 20th century. It does not aim to promote policies for the good of the agricultural industry - for that the reader may consult books such as 'Our Land, Our Food' by Sir Richard Body. However, there is a matter of policy, discussed by Sir Richard in his book, which I encountered while working for MAFF and which I can touch upon here. This is the system of 'organic' farming, as it has come to be called. We were actually farming in this way at the D'Urbans farm before World War II, though perhaps our use of copper sulphate as a seed dressing might have disqualified us, in strict Soil Association terms, from membership of the modern club.

In 1987, at a time when surplus production was becoming a problem in the E E C, I visited a well-known organic farm and wrote an article about it which was published in Crops magazine, Vol 4, No. 5. The following is an extract from that article.

BACK TO OLD-STYLE FARMING.

Mr Barry Wookey has been giving organic farming a try since 1970 on a 668 ha farm at Rushall in Wiltshire.

He has returned to the old system of mixed farming and to almost forgotten techniques such as bastard fallows and stale seed beds to control weeds and retain soil fertility.

He is working to an eight-course rotation as follows: Year 1: long ley, grazed: 2: long ley grazed: 3: long ley hay and bastard fallow: 4: winter wheat: 5: winter wheat undersown with ryegrass and red clover: 6: short ley, hay and bastard fallow: 7: winter wheat undersown red clover grazed with sheep and ploughed in February: 8: spring corn undersown to long ley.

Mr Wookey took me round the farm last summer. His crops were thin by modern standards and he acknowledges that his average yields are about half those obtained by the high-tech systems. He goes for longer-strawed wheats such as Maris Wigeon [which he has cut with a binder for thatching straw] as an aid in suppressing weeds. His crops were not dirty although he does have the odd disaster with poppies or charlock. If wild oats are very bad he is prepared to make hay of the crop - otherwise he hand rogues.

How can a system like his pay? Well, his variable costs are low, and the wheat is normally sold at a premium price under the Soil Association label.

Mr Wookey has installed a 36-inch Simon Barron stone flour mill on the farm and has a regular outlet for his baking quality wheat as organically grown flour.

He calculates that, by adding value in this way, he can increase the gross margin per hectare of wheat.

Gross margins on the wheat land look good - but half the arable farm is in long and short leys. These are stocked with Friesian cross Hereford steers and a breeding flock of mule ewes

He reckons that grassland gross margins from conventional and organic systems, with his type of livestock and making allowance for his premium prices, are roughly similar. But they are obviously much lower than for cash cereals

Mr Wookey's system seems to be viable under his conditions, although he insists that it should still be regarded as experimental. However, if only a small percentage of farmers halved their yields by going organic, the problem of E E C surpluses would be greatly reduced or eliminated.

So why are the authorities so contemptuous of organic farming?

The future will depend on the proportion of consumers who are prepared to pay sufficiently extra for their food and drink to balance the higher cost of organic production.

As Mr Wookey pointed out, the extra cost of the food would be no more than we all pay to support the price of the same foods under the Common Agricultural Policy of the EEC. Organic farming would be good for rural employment, too,. But for some of us it will mean bending the back once more over the hoe and waving goodbye to the spray boom.

The above article was written 17 years ago, and there have been some changes. Mr Nigel Wookey, Barry's son who now manages the farm, tells me that it is still run in the old mixed farming, 'organic', manner - but, like so many other farms, Rushall has taken on a considerable area of extra land in order to remain viable.

Nigel Wookey still believes in the future of organic farming, but he feels that the system needs to be tightly controlled, particularly when it comes to the importation of 'organic' produce from overseas sources which may not have been fully checked. He also feels that the public needs to be better informed of the virtues of organically produced food. Lip service is still paid in many quarters to the virtues of non-chemical, organic farm production, but the vast majority of the public continues to buy food on price and will not pay for the extra cost of old-fashioned methods. Organic food sales are today no more than 2 per cent of the total.

25

Return to Framlingham

I recently went back to Framlingham after many years, prepared to suffer the mixed feelings of nostalgia. In fact, the centre of the town had hardly changed over half a century, though it looked more prosperous than it did in the thirties, with the market square newly paved and the Crown Hotel promoting itself in gilded lettering. The flint stone tower of St Michael's Church no longer chimed 'Home Sweet Home' every four hours but I went inside and little had changed. The verger told me about some of the personalities of my youth but few seemed to have survived. He did not know about Carrie Smith and I had to point out to him the oak pews with their carved inscription which said that they had been bequeathed by Caroline Smith. Her story paints a fragment of the town's social history.

Carrie Smith was a spinster of some standing and we knew her well. She was the daughter of a harness maker in the town [William Smith, listed under 'traders', 1871 Census, in A History of Framlingham by Muriel L Kilvert] and she decided at an early age to leave home and seek her fortune in the empire. She found herself in Vancouver when the sidewalks were of timber slats and the great expansion was beginning. She opened a milliners shop when ladies' hats were real embellishments and ostrich feathers abounded on them.

Carrie Smith made a small fortune in British Columbia but she had never forgotten her roots and she came home to Framlingham in the 1930s to enjoy her well-earned retirement. She seemed to have no surviving relatives in the town but she found accommodation there and this included long periods as 'paying guest' at our D'Urbans farm at a time when 'diversification', as they now call it, was needed to keep the farm solvent. She was socially inclined and helped, I remember, to run Koon Can parties in the town and at our farm. From time to time she would disappear to Wiesbaden or Bath to take the waters or to Weston-super-mare or some Swiss resort. She walked everywhere using a stick emblazoned with continental badges and wore steel-rimmed glasses over her long, pointed nose.

She had obviously been careful with money all her life but I well remember that she gave me a second-hand Hercules bicycle [they cost £3 19s 11d new in those days] for my fifteenth birthday.

After we left Framlingham she went back on a visit to Vancouver and I have been able, through the courtesy of the present archivist of that city, to obtain a few details of her life there. It appears that she visited the archives office and the first city archivist, Major J S Matthews, made the following notes about her visit.

" .... a most charming and vivacious old lady, she must have been a regular prima donna in her day. She called at the city archives today, 23rd November, 1943, to look around. 'I came to Vancouver', she said, 'in 1894 Father said, why cannot you stay at home? But I wanted to go.' And she clenched her gloved hand. 'I came here first to the leading dry goods store ... to be milliner. Before investing. To see what was what. Then I opened my own store on Hastings Street. .....I had the biggest millinery store in town, [with some emphasis] I had sometimes as many as fifteen girls.' Miss Smith talked of many old pioneers and evidently was acquainted with the elite in early Vancouver."

A regular churchgoer, she bequeathed a number of fine oak pews to St. Michael's Church, Framlingham. These are her memorial but there must be few indeed who can now recall this daughter of the town.

It was good to find Carley's grocery prospering. They advertise Traditional Suffolk Fayre, but they sell far more packaged foods than erstwhile; in offering a local delivery service they make no advance on pre-war practice. The Condul cafe has long since disappeared but the town has kept up with modernity in the shape of an excellent pizzeria, with Italian chef, on Castle Street, a Chinese takeaway and a fish bar on College Road. The busy public library is still there, but there is also a shop offering 'back up for all your computer needs' - a facility I could never have dreamt of when I went to borrow a Freya Stark or other travel book for my father. The old Spring pump still stands where it always stood, but no-one needs it now, since the public services — mains water, sewage, electricity and even a public convenience — came to the town after World War II.

Framlingham is still well served for schools but, a sign of the times, I found that the College now has quite a high intake of oriental students as compared with just two Burmese boys in my day.

The football, bowls, Young Farmers and other clubs are flourishing, though the F A D S is in temporary decline. Needless to say the Castle still stands and shelters a good museum, but the town is no longer the terminus of the railway branch line from Wickham Market which closed in 1965.

We always thought that Framlingham was an exceptionally fair and pleasant parish and now this has been confirmed. It finished among the top ten in a recent survey commissioned by Country Life magazine of the best places to live in Britain*. The survey was wide ranging and the marking was based on more than a dozen criteria focused on measured data. Local amenities such as those noted above figure among the criteria and it is interesting for me to record that the fine open air swimming bath at the College, installed in 1873, where I learned to swim, is now open to all town residents.

The story of the farms in the parish follows the national trend. There were 26 farmers listed in Kelley's Directory in 1937 and they were generally small by present day standards. Even before World War II many of them were occupied by families which had other sources of income. I am indebted to Edmund Brown, grandson of the farmer at Hill Farm, and an agricultural consultant in the area, for information on the state of farming in the parish of Framlingham. Today, although most of the units remain, they are often run in amalgamation with other farms, the

farmhouses used as residences by business men, or else they depend sub-
stantially on various forms of diversification. The D'Urbans farm has
diversified to an extraordinary extent. The latest Ordnance Survey map
still shows the 'Gull' but a large building marked 'Works' now covers the
area of the old farm buildings and yard. This is where the present occupiers - the Western Brothers - manufacture farm machinery which is
sold all over the world. When I visited I saw that many of the work force
were housed in caravans on the old Velvets meadow. Getting sufficient
trained local labour has been a difficulty and some of the work has been
out sourced to Lithuania! What would my father have made of that? The
farm itself, still 186 acres, is too small to be run economically on its own
and is now farmed in conjunction with two other local farms - and even
after spreading their overheads in this way, they find it necessary to use
some of their machinery on outside contract work.

*We go in search of quality of life." Sandy Mitchell, Country Life .
October 31, 2002

26

Reflections

Turning back to the Introduction to this book, I see that I was quoting Shakespeare and his farmer who hanged himself in the expectation of plenty. When reflecting on this, I, by chance, turned up some excerpts from an article in the June 1955 issue of the American magazine, Fortune. There were no photocopiers in those days, but I was so impressed with the article entitled, The Magnificent Decline of U S Farming, that I made a typed copy of it, using my old Remington portable, and the following are some paragraphs.

A fundamental measure of any civilisation is what it can produce besides enough to eat. .

Modern civilisation has learned how to reduce progressively the effort that man must devote to winning his daily bread.

1930 25% of U S population were farmers.

1955 13,5% " " " " " "

1955 Production 54% greater than in 1930 but average farmer capital investment in land and equipment 65% greater than in 1930.

A considerable decline in the number of inefficient, or marginal, farms is expected. On the other hand it is expected that the number of hobby or sideline suburban farms will increase from 1,700,000 to 2,000,000

Sooner or later, rising efficiency will bring the day when farm policy addresses itself to what must be its real aim in a dynamic America: the transformation of every genuine farmer into a highly capitalised, highly productive, highly specialised, prosperous professional entrepreneur.

How does the picture look now, half a century on from that Fortune article? One wonders what the writer would make of the current position in the U K where fewer than 2% of the working population are now immediately engaged in agriculture.

Has the great drop in the proportion of the population working in food production led to a commensurate improvement in our 'civilisation',with all its production of cars, computers, publications, holidays and the other paraphernalia of the modern age? Would we be happier if we made a small U-turn back in the direction of work on the land?. And where do the 'developing' countries stand in all this, with their high percentage of the population chained to subsistence agriculture.?

As mentioned in the chapter on the Small Farmer Scheme, in the paragraph on allotments, there still seems to be some hankering after work close to the land, not least among people confined in air-conditioned offices for much of their lives, though this is still far from heralding a widespread return to uneconomic 'yeoman' farming.

The 'Fortune' prediction that there would be a big increase in part time small farms, dependent for survival on diversification, has come true, as has their other prediction that 'genuine' farmers will have to be highly specialised entrepreneurs in order to survive. This is the picture we are seeing now in the U K and describes most modern intensive livestock and horticultural holdings and those arable farms which have kept going by greatly expanding their acreage.* It is not an industry providing a livelihood for a host of small farmers without whom, John Hare declared, 'the whole country would be immeasurably poorer'.

See: Farm Modernisation and the Countryside: the impact of increasing field size and hedge removal on arable farming. Ford Sturrock & John Cathie. University of Cambridge Department of Land Economy, Occasional Paper No 12, 1980.

Henry Ford said that history was bunk and others have claimed that it does not repeat itself. But the story of recent farming history in this book is not bunk. Moreover, even within the twentieth century there are signs of agricultural history repeating itself and there may be lessons in this history which could be usefully studied when policies towards the land are considered.

I recently went back to the old windmill at Saxtead which used to grind our corn. It stopped commercial production in 1946 and now only turns to demonstrate to groups of visitors of whom there were 5,000 in 2002. But, *mirabile dictu,* windmills are now the flavour of the month, needed to generate electricity. This is not exactly a case of history repeating itself – there are better examples of that in the way public regard for agriculture has oscillated.

During the first world war the farming industry was held in high regard for the way it had increased production, spurred on by the government and Agricultural Executive Committees, so that the nation could feed itself through the years of the U-boat blockade. In recognition of this the government passed in 1917 the Corn Production Act which was to benefit farmer, landlords and workers by guaranteeing prices, rents and wages. Yet, after just four years, the act was repealed.

There followed the years of deep agricultural depression. The chairman of the Wheat Commission summed it up when he said, 'everyone knows that agriculture is a depressed industry. The world price of wheat is so low that it is hardly possible anywhere in the world to cultivate it at a profit'. The acreage of wheat in this country fell from about 2,000,000 in 1922 to some 1,200,000 in 1932. The farming industry was left to languish, but, when the second world war broke out, it found itself again in high favour. The 'doomsday' survey, the classification of all farms, the demand that every farm should increase production, ploughing and other production grants and the reinstatement of the War Agricultural Executive Committees - this was history repeating itself.

The turn of events following World War II did not repeat exactly the story of farming after 1918. There were the same glowing tributes to the way the industry had fed the nation through the dark days of the U-boat war, but this time a serious world food shortage continued for several years. Demands for greater food production increased and a plethora of grants and subsidies was showered on farming to encourage greater home food production. Farmers responded to the call and their effort was successful. Inevitably we found ourselves once more in an era of overproduction. Profits dropped or disappeared, many small farmers had to give up or kept going only with the help of drastic diversification, and there were actual cases of suicide because of the distress in the industry.

History repeated itself in the attitude taken by the government. In January 2000, Prime Minister Tony Blair at the National Farmers Union Annual General Meeting, assured *'agriculturists that they were not without sympathisers in the government ....the government could do little to help.'* But he urged his audience *'not to be too downhearted; agricultural prosperity would return'.* His speech writer must have turned back for inspiration to the remarks of a previous government spokesman, Arthur Boscawen, Minister for Agriculture, who said, in a speech to the National Farmers Union dinner, as reported in the Journal of the Ministry of Agriculture, November 1922, *'Agriculture was certainly going through a critical time and he had the greatest sympathy with all classes engaged in it. The government was powerless to act ...... this he knew was cold comfort but ...... the industry must work out its own salvation'.*

Yes, history repeating itself, but with a difference. In the general depression of the 1930s landlords had difficulty in finding tenants for some farms and owner occupiers often could not find buyers when wishing to sell. In these post-World War II years there is the paradox that farm prices are high. Farms are now often within commuting range for businessmen who do not suffer from the deep general depression which characterised the 20s and 30s and have money to buy and enjoy the cachet of country living and do not depend upon income from the farm.

There was another factor, too, which supported the farming condition after World War II – the advent of the European Economic Commission [EEC] and the Common Agricultural Policy [CAP]. Agriculture being relatively more important in EEC countries, it has attracted more support there than it would have done in an isolated U K. But even the CAP was unable to maintain European farm prices in the face of world competition and we entered the era of set-aside when farms were paid to take a proportion of their land out of production. Some forms of production are protected by import duties and, if there is overproduction, the surplus can be exported with support from export levies, clearly disadvantaging third world producers.

Financial assistance is now paid in a bewildering variety of ways to farmers who observe certain environmental rules. Oliver Walston, farmer and writer, has headed his recent article in the Daily Telegraph about the current systems of grant aid, 'Last year I was a farmer, this year I'm a park keeper'. David Richardson, a respected columnist in the Farmers Weekly, wrote in their January 9 -15, 0004 issue: 'We are now perceived as spongers and pariahs who receive far too much of the nation's cash'.

So, can we learn something from my story of farming in the 20th century? It looks as though history has repeated itself, but with considerable diversions. The history of farming in this period is certainly not 'bunk' and lessons can be learned from it. You do not have to be a cynic to look back with understanding at Shakespeare's farmer who hanged himself in the expectation of plenty. It seems that the farmer's status in the community remains where it was three hundred years ago – well regarded only when food is scarce.

Selected Bibliography

Atkinson, Rev. J C. British Birds, Eggs and Nests. Routledge, 1862.

Body, Sir Richard. Our Food, Our Land. Rider, 1991.

Brown, Jonathan. Farm Machinery, 1750 - 1945. Batsford,1989.

Buxbaum, Tim. Pargeting. Shire, 1999.

Cherrington, John. On the Smell of an Oily Rag. Farming Press,1979.

Farmhouse Fare. Hulton Press Ltd. For Farmers Weekly Ltd. 1944.

Howard. Sir Albert. An Agricultural Testament, Oxford University Press, 1956.

Kilvert, Muriel L.A. History of Framlingham. Bolton and Price, 1995.

Reader's Digest. Yesterday's Britain, Reader's Digest Assn. Ltd. 1998

Soper M R H. Years of Change. Farming Press, 1995.

Staniforth, A R. Straw and Straw Craftsmen. Shire, 1991.

Sturrock, Ford & Cathie, John. Farm Mechanisation and the Countryside. University of Cambridge Dept. of Land Economy, 1980.

Twinch, Carol. Tythe War. Old Pond, 2001

Press & Periodicals
Journal of Ministry of Agriculture. October 1922 and later numbers.

East Anglian Daily Times, June, 1995.

The Oldie, October, 1999.

Daily Telegraph, W F Deede's column, 7 July, 0004.

Standard Cyclopedia of Modern Agriculture. Gresham, 1910.

White's Directory of Lincolnshire, 1892.

Farmers Weekly, 24 Feb 0003 and 15 Jan 0004.

The Independent, 21 Feb 2001.

Country Life, Oct 31,2002

Fortune Magazine, June, 1955.

Agricultural Progress, Jubilee Edition, Vol. 50, 1975.

FARM SURVEY

County .... Code No. ....
District .... Parish ....
Name of holding .... Name of farmer ....
Address of farmer ....
Number and edition of 6-inch Ordnance Survey Sheet containing farmstead ....

A. TENURE.

1. Is occupier tenant ... ...
   owner ... ...
2. If tenant, name and address of owner :—
   ....
   ....
   ....

3. Is farmer full time farmer ... ...
   part time farmer ... ...
   spare time farmer ... ...
   hobby farmer ... ...
   other type ... ...
   Other occupation, if any :—

	Yes	No
4. Does farmer occupy other land ?		

Name of Holding	County	Parish

	Yes	No
5. Has farmer grazing rights over land not occupied by him ?		

If so, nature of such rights ...
....
....

B. CONDITIONS OF FARM.

	Heavy	Medium	Light	Peaty
1. Proportion (%) of area on which soil is				

2. Is farm conveniently laid out ?	Yes ...	
	Moderately	
	No ...	

	Good	Fair	Bad
3. Proportion (%) of farm which is naturally			
4. Situation in regard to road ...			
5. Situation in regard to railway ...			
6. Condition of farmhouse			
Condition of buildings ...			
7. Condition of farm roads			
8. Condition of fences			
9. Condition of ditches			
10. General condition of field drainage			
11. Condition of cottages			

	No.
12. Number of cottages within farm area ...	
Number of cottages elsewhere	
13. Number of cottages let on service tenancy ...	

	Yes	No
14. Is there infestation with :—		
rabbits and moles		
rats and mice		
rooks and wood pigeons ...		
other birds		
insect pests		
15. Is there heavy infestation with weeds ?		

C. WATER AND ELECTRICITY.

	Pipe	Well	Roof	Stream	None
Water supply :—					
1. To farmhouse ...					
2. To farm buildings ...					
3. To fields ...					

	Yes	No
4. Is there a seasonal shortage of water ? ...		
Electricity supply :—		
5. Public light		
Public power		
Private light		
Private power		
6. Is it used for household purposes ? ...		
Is it used for farm purposes ? ...		

D. MANAGEMENT.

1. Is farm classified as A, B or C ?		
2. Reasons for B or C :—		
old age		
lack of capital		
personal failings		

If personal failings, details :—
....
....
....

	Good	Fair	Poor	Bad
3. Condition of arable land ...				
4. Condition of pasture ...				

	Adequate	To some extent	Not at all
5. Use of fertilisers on :—			
arable land ...			
grass land ...			

Field information recorded by
....

Date of recording ....

ISBN 141205534-2

9 781412 055345